Share With Love:
Canadian Cooking

by
Joyce Holt

Order this book online at www.trafford.com
or email orders@trafford.com

Most Trafford titles are also available at major online book retailers.

Note for Librarians: A cataloguing record for this book is available from Library
and Archives Canada at www.collectionscanada.ca/amicus/index-e.html

Printed in Victoria, BC, Canada.

ISBN: 978-1-4269-1248-1

*Our mission is to efficiently provide the world's finest, most comprehensive
book publishing service, enabling every author to experience success.
To find out how to publish your book, your way, and have it available
worldwide, visit us online at www.trafford.com*

Trafford rev. 09/17/09

www.trafford.com

North America & international
toll-free: 1 888 232 4444 (USA & Canada)
phone: 250 383 6864 ♦ fax: 812 355 4082

Acknowledgement

I've been saving recipes for years thinking that maybe one day they would go into a book and now is the time. I am grateful for the help of my daughter Gail and my husband Walter; I couldn't have done this without their love and encouragement; they made my wish come true! I hope you will enjoy this book as much as I have enjoyed putting it together

Joyce Holt
May 9, 2009

Contents

DESSERTS

PIES & PASTRY

PRESERVES

SALADS

Coleslaw

2 cups	Shredded cabbage
½ cup	Diced cucumber
½ cup	Diced celery
¼ cup	Green pepper, chopped
2 small	Green onions, chopped
1 tsp	Salt
¼ tsp	Paprika
½ cup	Salad dressing or mayonnaise
1 Tbsp	Vinegar
1 tsp	Prepared mustard

- Combine vegetables, chill for about 30 minutes
- Combine the remaining ingredients in a separate bowl
- Pour over the cooled vegetables, toss lightly
- Chill again
- Garnish with 1 – 2 tsp pimento

Serves 4 - 6

Broccoli Salad

2 cups	Broccoli cut into florets
2 cups	Cauliflower cut into florets
½ small	Red onion, sliced into rings
¼ cup	Sunflower seeds
¼ cup	Sliced almonds
½ cup	Raisins, washed and dried
½ cup	Mayonnaise
1 Tbsp	Sugar
1 Tbsp	White wine vinegar

- Combine vegetables, sunflower seeds, almonds and raisins
- Combine mayonnaise, sugar and wine vinegar
- Toss dressing and vegetables together
- Cover and refrigerate for at least 2 hours

This salad keeps very well, up to 1 week in the fridge

Serves 6 - 8

Jellied Salad

3 cups	Cabbage, shredded
½ cup	Raisins
½ cup	Carrot, grated
¼ cup	Mayonnaise
1 cup	Apple, chopped
1 pkg	Lime Jell-o powder
1 Tbsp	Vinegar

- Combine all ingredients except Jell-o powder and vinegar
- Using a separate bowl, follow the directions on the Jell-o box less 2 Tbsp of water, then add vinegar
- Let the Jell-o set slightly then add the remaining ingredients
- Transfer to a jelly mould and chill until set

Serves 4 – 6

This salad is perfect for an afternoon luncheon as an accompaniment for cold cuts and fruit.

Variation: lemon Jell-o could be used in place of lime

3-Bean Salad

1 – 14 oz can	Cut green beans, drained and rinsed
1 – 14 oz can	Cut yellow beans, drained and rinsed
1 – 19 oz can	Red kidney beans drained and rinsed
1 small	Red onion, thinly sliced
1 cup	Celery, diced
1 small	Green pepper, diced
½ cup	White sugar
1/3 cup	Vegetable oil
½ tsp	Salt, or to taste
½ tsp	Pepper, or to taste
1/3 cup	White vinegar

- Combine all the vegetables
- Mix sugar, vinegar, vegetable oil, salt and pepper
- Toss together and chill

Serves 6 - 8

Potato Salad

7 medium	Potatoes
¼ cup	Celery, chopped
¼ cup	Green onion, chopped
¼ cup	Radish, chopped
4 eggs	Hard boiled
2 tsp	Mustard
½ tsp	Celery salt
½ - ¾ cup	Mayonnaise
Dash	White pepper
¾ tsp	Salt

- Boil the potatoes with 1 tsp of salt until tender, drain
- Peel and cut potatoes into small cubes
- In a large bowl combine potatoes, three of the eggs chopped, chopped celery, onions and radish
- Dressing: combine mustard, celery salt, white pepper, mayonnaise and salt together
- Add dressing to vegetables, toss well and garnish with remaining boiled egg, sliced

Serves 6 – 8

Romaine Salad

1	Romaine lettuce, cleaned and torn into bite-sized pieces
1 cup	Grape tomatoes
½ cup	Celery, chopped
¼ cup	Green onion, chopped
1 cup	Red or green grapes, halved
2 Tbsp	Chives, chopped
½ tsp	Dried mint
2 Tbsp	Red wine vinegar
2 Tbsp	Olive oil
2 tsp	Sugar
	Salt and pepper to taste

- In a salad bowl, combine lettuce, grape tomatoes, chopped celery, chopped onions, grapes and chives
- In small bowl whisk together wine vinegar, sugar, salt & pepper, dried mint and olive oil until well blended
- Pour dressing over the lettuce mixture, toss lightly and serve immediately

Serves 6 - 8

Carrot Salad

3 cups	Carrots, shredded
1 cup	Raisins
½ cup	Mayonnaise
2 Tbsp	Lemon juice
2 Tbsp	Vegetable oil
2 Tbsp	White sugar
	Salt and pepper to taste

- Place shredded carrots into a salad bowl
- Soak raisins in hot water until plump, squeeze out excess water, then add to shredded carrots
- In separate bowl, combine remaining ingredients to make dressing
- Add dressing to the carrots and raisins and mix thoroughly
- Chill for about one hour

Serves 4 – 6

Melon Salad

3 cups	Cantaloupe, cut into ¾" pieces or in balls
3 cups	Watermelon, cut into ¾" pieces or in balls
2 medium	English cucumbers, sliced
½ cup	Vegetable oil
¼ cup	Lemon juice
1 tsp	Sugar
½ tsp	Salt

- In a large bowl, mix the oil, lemon juice, sugar, salt and whisk together
- Add melons and cucumbers then toss gently
- Cover and refrigerate for at least two hours
- Drain and serve

Serves 6 – 8

Serving suggestion: Line a flat bowl with lettuce leaves, place drained salad on top and garnish with thinly sliced oranges

Spinach Salad

6 cups	Spinach, torn into bite sized pieces
1 rib	Celery, diced
2	Green onions, diced
3 large	Mushrooms, sliced
3	Eggs, hard cooked and sliced
6 slices	Bacon, cooked crisp & broken into pieces
4 Tbsp	Mayonnaise-type salad dressing
2 Tbsp	Red wine vinegar
2 tsp	Sugar
	Salt and pepper, to taste

- In a salad bowl, mix spinach, celery, onions, mushrooms, eggs and bacon together, toss lightly
- In separate bowl combine mayonnaise, vinegar, sugar, salt and pepper, mix well
- Add to salad mixture and toss together
- Serve immediately

Serves 6 - 8

Baby Greens Salad

1/3 cup	Glazed walnuts, broken into pieces
3 cups	Baby greens
½ small	Red onion, sliced
½ cup	Dried cranberries
½ cup	Gorgonzola cheese, cubed
¼ tsp	Dry mustard
¼ tsp	Salt
2 Tbsp	White sugar
1 Tbsp	Vinegar
¼ cup	Vegetable oil
1 Tbsp	Mayonnaise
2 tsp	Water

- Prepare glazed walnuts (allow 1 hour to dry)
- Combine baby greens, sliced red onions, glazed walnuts dried cranberries and cubed gorgonzola, set aside
- Make dressing: mix mustard, salt, sugar, vinegar, vegetable oil, mayonnaise and water in blender
- Pour dressing over mixed greens, toss gently
- Serve immediately

Glazed walnuts

Place ½ cup sugar in small saucepan over medium heat. Add ¼ cup water and heat stirring constantly until sugar is dissolved. Add approximately 1 cup of walnuts and toss until coated. Remove walnuts and place on foil until dry. Remaining walnuts can be stored in the fridge in an airtight container
Serves 4 – 6

Spinach Mold Salad

¼ cup	Cold water
10 ounces	Beef broth
2 envelopes	Unflavoured gelatine
¼ tsp	Salt
2 Tbsp	Lemon juice
1 cup	Mayonnaise
1 medium	Onion, quartered
1 - 10 oz pkg	Frozen spinach, thawed
4 eggs	Hard boiled, peel and quarter
½ pound	Cooked bacon, crumbled

- Pour cold water and ¼ cup of the beef broth into a blender container, sprinkle with the gelatine, let stand until gelatine softens
- Heat remaining beef broth in saucepan until boiling
- Add hot beef broth to blender, cover and process at low speed until gelatine is dissolved using rubber spatula to push gelatine granules into the mixture
- Add salt, lemon juice and mayonnaise, process until well blended
- Add onion, cover and process at high speed until onion is chopped
- Add spinach and eggs, cover and process lightly until eggs are chopped, do not over process!
- Stir in the bacon, then turn in to a 6 – cup mold
- Chill until firm

Serves 8

Carrot Mold

1 ½ cups	Orange juice
2 envelopes	Unflavoured gelatine
½ cup	Boiling orange juice
¼ tsp	Salt
1 cup	Mayonnaise
1 ½ cups	Carrot, diced small
1 – 13 oz can	Crushed pineapple, undrained
½ cup	Dried cranberries

- Pour ½ cup cold orange juice into blender container; sprinkle gelatine, let stand for 5 minutes
- Add boiling orange juice and process at low speed until gelatine is dissolved
- Push gelatine granules into the mixture using rubber spatula
- Add remaining cold orange juice, salt and mayonnaise and blend well
- Add carrots, cover then process at high speed until carrots are finely grated
- Stir in the pineapple and cranberries
- Pour into a 6 – cup mold, chill until firm
- Unfold onto a serving plate

Serves 8

Cabbage Salad

4 cups	Cabbage, thinly sliced
1 tsp	Onion, minced
1½ Tbsp	Green pepper, finely sliced
2 tsp	Sugar
1 tsp	Dried dill
2 Tbsp	Olive oil
3 Tbsp	Vinegar

• Mix all ingredients together add salt and pepper to taste
Variations:
   Add ½ cup of any one of the following:
   Raisins
   Dried cranberries
   Chopped black olives

Serves 6 – 8

Chick Pea Salad

1 – 19 oz can	Chick Peas, drained & rinsed well
1 – 10 oz can	Whole mushrooms, drained
½ small	Red onion, sliced
1 small	Clove garlic, minced
12	Black olives, halved
1 ½ Tbsp	Olive oil

- Mix all ingredients together add salt and pepper to taste then sprinkle with dried basil

Serves 4

SOUPS

Leek & Potato Soup

3	Leeks, cleaned and chopped
1 cup	Mashed potatoes (2 – 3 potatoes)
2½ cups	Water from boiling potatoes
3 Tbsp	Butter
6 Tbsp	Flour
¾ cup	Milk
¼ cup	Cream

- Peel then boil the potatoes; drain, reserving 2½ cups of the water
- Mash the potatoes and set aside
- Melt the butter, add flour and mix well
- Add the potato water slowly and stir constantly until thickened
- Add chopped leeks and mashed potatoes then bring to a boil
- Add the milk ¼ cup at a time
- To prevent from curdling, do not boil after adding milk
- Top with ¼ cup of cream

Serves 4

Pea Soup

2 quarts	Water
2 cups	Dried green split peas
1 rib	Celery, coarsely chopped
1 large	Carrot, chopped
1 small	Onion, chopped
1 pinch	Cayenne pepper
1	Bay leaf
1 tsp	Salt
¼ tsp	White pepper

- Combine all ingredients in large saucepan and boil together hard for 20 minutes
- Reduce heat and simmer until the peas are tender
- Strain through a fine sieve
- Reheat to boiling point

Serves 8

Butternut Squash Soup

2 Tbsp	Butter
1 medium	Onion, minced
3 cups	Butternut squash, peeled, seeded, cubed
1 ¼ quarts	Chicken broth
1 ½ cups	Potatoes, peeled and cubed
½ cup	Whipping cream
1 ½ Tbsp	Green onion, finely chopped
	Salt and pepper to taste

- Melt butter in large saucepan, add onions and cook until soft, about 5 minutes
- Add squash, potatoes, chicken stock and bring to a boil, reduce heat to low
- Cover and simmer for about 35 minutes until vegetables are soft
- Pour soup into a blender and blend until smooth
- Return soup to saucepan and stir in the cream, season with salt and pepper and reheat slowly
- Stir in green onion just before serving

Serves 6 – 8

Tomato Soup

1 – 20 oz can	Tomato juice
2½ cups	Milk
4 Tbsp	Butter
4 Tbsp	Flour
¼ tsp	Baking soda
	Salt to taste

- Add tomato juice to medium saucepan, bring just to the boil
- In another saucepan create a white sauce
  - Melt butter and add flour and mix to a paste
  - Add milk slowly, stir until thickened
  - Add salt
- Add baking soda to the tomato juice, this will cause the juice to foam, stir until the foam goes down
- Once foam has gone down, slowly add the tomato juice mixture to the white sauce
- Stir well after each addition

Serves 4

Chicken Noodle Soup

10	Chicken thighs
8 cups (approx)	Water
2	Bay leaves
1 Tbsp	Salt
½ cup	Onion, diced
½ pkg. (340gr)	Egg noodles, cooked & rinsed
1 tsp	Chicken fat

- Make chicken stock
  - Cover chicken thighs with cold water, bring to a boil then skim off the foam
  - Add salt then simmer (1½ - 2 hours) - do not boil
  - Remove chicken then strain stock
  - Return chicken to stock then cool
- Skim fat from top of cooled stock, saving 1 tsp
- Remove chicken from stock and remove meat from the bones
- Return stock and chicken to a clean pot
- Add bay leaf and simmer for ½ hour
- Melt the 1 tsp of chicken fat in a small saucepan, add the diced onion, cook for one minute then add to the stock
- Add cooked & rinsed noodles and chicken to the stock
- Adjust salt and pepper

Serves 6

French Onion Soup

1 Tbsp	Butter
2 Tbsp	Good oil, olive or canola
4 large	Onions, sliced ¼ - ½ inch thick
4	Garlic cloves
1 tsp	Sugar
2 Tbsp	Flour
½ cup	White wine
2¼ quarts	Beef stock
6 – 8 slices	French bread, thickly sliced
3 cups	Swiss cheese, grated

- In a large saucepan, heat butter and oil over medium heat, Add onions and cook for 10 – 15 minutes until they begin to brown
- Chop 3 garlic cloves and add to the onions
- Add the sugar and continue cooking until the onions are brown, stirring often
- Sprinkle flour over onions and blend well
- Stir in the wine and the beef broth and bring to a boil then skim off any foam
- Lower heat and simmer for 45 minutes
- Toast the bread and rub each slice with remaining garlic clove
- Place 6 - 8 flame proof bowls on cookie sheet
- Fill each bowl ¾ full, top with a piece of toast and top with grated cheese
- Broil about 4 minutes, until cheese starts to melt.

Serves 8

Wonton Soup

1 cup	Ground pork
1 tsp	Sugar
1 Tbsp	Rice wine
1 Tbsp	Soy sauce
1 Tbsp	Onion, minced
1 tsp	Fresh ginger, minced
24	Wonton wrappers
4 cups	Chicken broth
	Green onions finely chopped

- In a bowl mix pork, sugar, rice wine, soy sauce, minced onion and ginger
- Set aside for about ½ hour
- Place rounded tsp of pork mixture in centre of each wonton wrapper
- Wet edges of each filled wrapper
- Bring the four corners together and twist gently creating a sealed pouch
- Bring chicken broth to a rolling boil in pot or wok
- Add wontons and boil for 6 – 8 minutes
- Season with soy sauce and chopped green onions

Serves 8

Clam Chowder

2 – 14 oz can	Baby clams
1 – 16 oz can	Clam juice
4 slices	Bacon
1 large	Onion
3 medium	Potatoes, cubed
2 ribs	Celery, chopped
½ tsp	Salt
¼ tsp	White pepper
1½ - 2 cups	Milk
2 Tbsp	Flour

- Fry bacon, remove from pan and cut up
- Add onion and celery to bacon fat and sauté for 5 minutes
- Add potato cubes, salt & pepper and chopped bacon
- Add flour and stir
- Add clam juice
- Cook 15 – 20 minutes or until vegetables are tender
- Add clams and cook 4 minutes longer
- Add milk and heat through – do not boil

Serves 4

Lettuce Soup

1 cup	Chopped onions
2 cloves	Garlic, chopped
4 Tbsp	Butter
¾ tsp	Salt
¼ tsp	Pepper
¾ cup	Potato, peeled and diced
½ cup	Celery leaves, chopped
8 cups	Romaine lettuce, chopped
3 cups	Chicken broth

- In a large heavy saucepan over low heat, cook onion and garlic in 2 Tbsp of the butter, stirring until softened
- Add salt and pepper
- Stir in potato, celery leaves, lettuce and chicken broth, bring to a boil
- Reduce heat, cover and simmer until potato is very tender (about 10 minutes)
- In a blender puree soup in batches (Be careful when blending hot liquids)
- Transfer to a clean saucepan, bring to a simmer
- Whisk in remaining 2 Tbsp butter

Serves 4

Carrot Soup

2 Tbsp	Butter
1 cup	Chopped onion
2 cloves	Garlic, minced
1 stock	Celery, chopped
6	Carrots, peeled and sliced
1	Potato, peeled and cubed
4 cups	Chicken or vegetable broth
½ cups	Cream

- Melt butter in large saucepan, add onions, garlic and celery, cook until soft
- Add remaining ingredients, lower heat and cook until vegetables are tender
- Puree in a blender
- Add the cream just before serving

Serves 3 – 4

Beef Barley Soup

9 cups	Beef broth
4 stocks	Celery, cut into ½ inch pieces
3	Carrots, peeled and chopped
1 large	Onion, chopped
4	Garlic cloves, chopped
3	Bay leaves
1/3 cup	Barley, rinsed
	Salt and pepper to taste

- Combine all ingredients in heavy sauce pan, bring to a boil
- Reduce heat to medium-low
- Cover and simmer for 1 hour, stirring occasionally
- Season with salt and pepper

Serves 4

Borscht

1 large	Onion, chopped
3 Tbsp	Vegetable oil
1 Tbsp	Butter
2 cloves	Garlic, minced
3 cups	Cabbage, chopped
2 medium	Potatoes, peeled and diced
8 cups	Beef broth
6, 2" – 3"	Beets, peeled and diced
2 Tbsp	White wine vinegar
2 Tbsp	Dried dill weed
	Salt and pepper to taste

- Heat the butter and oil in a large pot over medium/high heat
- Add potatoes, cabbage and onion and sauté until cabbage softens (about 5 minutes)
- Add broth and the beets, bring to a boil
- Add wine vinegar and dill weed
- Simmer for about 25 minutes
- Add to serving bowls
- Garnish with sour cream and dill

Serves 6 – 8

Minestrone

4 Tbsp each	Butter and olive oil
1 small	Onion, chopped
½ cup	Leek, finely chopped (white part only)
4	Garlic cloves, chopped fine
1 cup	Carrot, cut in ½" dice
2 ribs	Celery, cut in ½" dice
2 small	Zucchini, cut in ½" dice
2 cups	Potato, cut in ½" dice
3 cups	Cabbage, shredded
1 – 28 oz can	Diced tomatoes, well drained
3 cups	Vegetable broth
1 – 19 oz can	White kidney beans, rinsed and drained well
¾ cup	Macaroni, cooked and drained
½ tsp	Dried basil
½ tsp each	Salt and pepper

- In a heavy pot, cook onions and leeks until soft
- Add carrot, celery, garlic and cook for about 4 minutes
- Add zucchini and potatoes, cook for 5 minutes stirring often
- Add cabbage, parsley, basil, salt and pepper and cook stirring until cabbage has wilted
- Add tomatoes and broth; bring to a boil, simmer 25 min.
- Add cooked macaroni and drained beans and cook for another 10 – 15 minutes
- Serve with crusty bread and parmesan cheese or parmesan herb crackers

Serves 6 – 8

Parmesan Herb Crackers

½ cup	Parmesan cheese
1 Tbsp	Finley chopped fresh parsley
1 Tbsp	Green onion, finely chopped
¼ tsp	Paprika

- Finely grate the parmesan cheese into small bowl, add remaining ingredients, mix to combine
- Drop by level teaspoon onto a non-stick cookie sheet
- Cook it under the broiler for 1 minute until golden and bubbling; watch closely as cheese burns easily
- Let crackers cool on the pan
- Carefully lift off with a spatula
- Eat within 2 – 3 hours, does not store well

Makes: 3 dozen

APPETIZERS

Stuffed Snow Peas

50	Young snow peas, try to get all the same size
8 ounces	Cream cheese
¼ cup	Green onion, finely chopped

- Blanch snow peas in lightly salted boiling water for 30 seconds. Immediately cool in ice water, then dry well
- Combine cream cheese and onion in a bowl
- Split the snow peas on the curved side and fill with cheese mixture

Serves 12 – 15

Smoked Salmon Mousse

8 ounces	Cream cheese
1/4 cup	Canned salmon, bones and skin removed
3 – 4 drops	Liquid smoke
	White pepper and salt to taste

- Combine all ingredients in a food processor, blend until smooth
- Chill 45 minutes to an hour

Yield approx 1-cup mousse

Serving suggestions:

Hollow out cherry tomatoes with a small baller or small spoon. Fill each tomato with mousse. Garnish with parsley and a thin slice of black olive

Place a Tbsp of mousse at the stem end of a Belgian endive leave. Garnish with thin slices of red pepper

Score a cucumber to create a striped effect then slice into 1-inch rounds. Using small melon baller or small spoon scoop out some of centre of each round. Spoon mousse into the cavity and garnish with either salmon roe or a small shrimp

Hot Crab Dip

8 ounces	Cream cheese
2 Tbsp	Milk
2 Tbsp	Green onion, finely chopped
½ tsp	Prepared mustard
¼ tsp	Salt
Dash	White pepper
1 – 7½ can	Crab meat, picked over rinsed & drained
1/3 cup	Flaked almonds

- Preheat oven to 375°F
- In a bowl beat cream cheese with the milk
- Add crab meat, onion, mustard, salt & pepper, blend well
- Spoon into a small oven proof bowl;
- Bake for 15 minutes
- Sprinkle almonds on top
- Return to oven and bake until cheese mixture is bubbly and the almonds are light golden colour 20 – 25 minutes
- Serve with melba toast, crackers or vegetables

Yield approx 1 ½ cup

Cheese Balls

1 pound	Goat cheese, at room temp
¼ cup	Cream cheese
¼ tsp	Salt
1 Tbsp	Green onion, minced
Coatings	See below

- Mix all ingredients together then roll into 1-inch balls
- Roll the balls in coating mix as follows:
- ¼ of the balls rolled in 3 – 4 Tbsp paprika
- ¼ of the balls rolled in 3 Tbsp coarsely ground black pepper
- ¼ of the balls rolled in 3 Tbsp ground walnuts
- ¼ of the balls rolled in 3 Tbsp sesame seeds

Serving suggestions:

1. Can be served on their own, or
2. Will greatly enhance a cheese platter or fruit tray

Tuna Stuffed Mushrooms

1-7oz can	Tuna, rinsed and drained
¼ cup	Soft bread crumbs
¼ cup	Mayonnaise
1 Tbsp	Shallot, finely chopped
1 tsp	Worcestershire sauce
18	Mushrooms, 1½" diameter

- Preheat oven to 375°F
- In a food processor combine the tuna, bread crumbs, mayonnaise, shallots, Worcestershire sauce and process until almost smooth
- Remove stems from mushrooms
- Spoon about 1 Tbsp of tuna mixture into centre of each mushroom cap
- Place in a shallow baking pan
- Cover with foil
- Bake 10 to 15 minutes or until hot

Yield 18

Salmon Pinwheels

4 ounces	Thinly sliced smoked salmon, or lox
1/4 cup	Sour cream
1 egg	Hard boiled then chopped
1 tsp	Chives, chopped
1/2 tsp	Horseradish
1 tsp	Lemon juice
2 Tbsp	Melted butter
2 – 10"	Soft tortilla shells
Garnish:	Black olives, chopped

- In a small bowl, coarsely chop salmon
- In a food processor combine chopped salmon, sour cream, egg, chives, horseradish, lemon juice and melted butter
- Process until mixture is almost smooth
- Spread each tortilla with half the salmon mixture
- Roll up tightly and wrap in plastic film
- Refrigerate for about 2 hours
- Just before serving, slice into 3/4 inch pieces
- Place cut side up on a serving plate and top with chopped olives

Yield approximately 2 dozen

Sesame Asparagus Rolls

20 slices	White bread, crusts removed
1 – 8 oz pkg	Cream cheese, softened
3 ounces	Blue cheese, crumbled
1	Egg, slightly beaten
20	Asparagus spears
1/3 cup	Margarine or butter
	Sesame seeds

- Preheat oven to 400°F
- Lightly grease cookie sheet
- Remove crusts from bread then flatten each slice with rolling pin
- In a small bowl combine the cheeses and egg
- Spread cheese mixture to edges of bread slices
- Remove woody end of asparagus and blanch in boiling water for 2 minutes, cool immediately, drain
- Trim asparagus to fit the bread
- Place one asparagus tip on each slice of bread
- Roll up jelly roll fashion
- Dip each roll in margarine or butter then roll in sesame seeds then cut into 3 equal pieces
- Place each piece cut side down on prepared cookie sheets and bake for 15 – 20 minutes or until light golden brown
- Serve warm

Yield 20

Curried Chicken Almond Rolls

1 cup	Finely chopped cooked chicken breast
1 cup	Mayonnaise
¾ cup	White cheddar or Monterey jack cheese, Shredded
1/3 cup	Almonds, finely chopped
¼ cup	Fresh finely chopped parsley
1 small	Onion, finely chopped
2 tsp	Curry powder
2 tsp	Lemon juice
½ tsp each	Salt and pepper
18 slices	White bread, crusts removed
¼ cup	Melted butter

- Preheat oven to 350°F
- Line cookie sheet with parchment or waxed paper
- Combine all ingredients except bread and butter in a small bowl, cover and refrigerate for 30 minutes
- Roll or flatten each slice of bread with a rolling pin
- Spread approx. 2 Tbsp of filling mixture on each piece of bread then roll up jelly roll fashion
- Secure with tooth picks then cut in half
- Place seam side down on prepared cookie sheet
- Brush with melted butter, and bake for 15 minutes

Yield 36 pieces

Pecan Canapés

18	Pecan halves
8 ounces	Light cream cheese at room temperature
½ cup	Ricotta cheese
¼ cup	Gorgonzola cheese at room temperature
1 Tbsp	Brandy
	Salt and pepper to taste
1	Baguette
	Butter

- Preheat oven to 375°F
- Chop pecans and set aside
- Combine cheeses and mash with a fork
- Add brandy and salt and pepper
- When it's smooth, add pecans and mix until well blended
- Cut baguette into 1/2" slices
- Butter each slice and place on baking sheet
- Bake baguette slices 8 – 10 minutes, then cool
- Spoon pecan mix onto each slice of baguette
- Garnish with orange zest

Yield 24 – 30 pieces

Nuts and Bolts

2 Tbsp	Butter
¼ tsp	Garlic salt
¼ tsp	Onion salt
2 tsp	Lemon juice
1 Tbsp	Worcestershire sauce
1 cup	Mixed nuts
1 cup	Pretzels
1 cup	Cheerios
1 cup	Shreddies
1 cup	Chex cereal
1 cup	Mini cheese sticks
1 cup	Crispix

- Preheat oven to 250°F
- Add butter to a 9" x 13" pan and melt in the oven
- Stir in garlic salt, onion salt, lemon juice, Worcestershire sauce and mix well
- Stir in nuts, pretzels and cereals and toss until well coated
- Bake at 250°F for 45 minutes stirring every 15 minutes
- Store in an airtight container

Yield 7 cups

Tortilla Rounds

25 medium	Shrimp, cooked & cleaned
2 medium	Avocados, ripe
1 tsp	Salt
	Cayenne to taste
2½ Tbsp	Lemon juice
½ cup	Cherry tomatoes, seeded and chopped
50	Round tortilla chips

- Cut shrimp in half lengthwise, set aside
- Peel and pit the avocadoes and in a bowl, mash them with a fork
- Add the salt, cayenne, lemon juice and tomatoes and combine well
- Just before serving, spread tortilla chips with avocado mixture
- Top mixture with half a shrimp
- Garnish each with a small parsley leaf

Yield approx 50

VEGETABLES

Baby Bok Choy with Bacon

2 pounds	Baby bok choy
2 Tbsp	Water
2 Tbsp	Sugar
2 Tbsp	White wine vinegar
2 tsp	Worcestershire sauce
1/4 cup	Chilli sauce
1 1/2 Tbsp	Vegetable oil
8 slices	Bacon, cooked and crumbled

- Break bok choy, wash well and drain
- Cut white stems into thin diagonal slices
- Cut the green tops into thicker slices
- Combine water, sugar, vinegar, Worcestershire, chilli sauce in a small sauce pan, heat
- Heat oil in a wok at medium high heat, add stems and stir fry until tender-crisp about 3 – 4 minutes
- Add leaves and stir fry 2 more minutes
- Place the bok choy on a serving dish,
- Spoon the sauce over top and sprinkle with bacon

6 servings

Carrots with Cranberries and Walnuts

1 pound	Carrots, peeled and sliced
1/3 cup	Beef broth
2 tsp	Shallots, chopped
½ tsp	Garlic, chopped
1/3 cup	Dried cranberries
1/3 cup	Walnuts, chopped and toasted
1 Tbsp	Butter

- Place carrots and broth in a sauté pan
- Add the shallots, garlic and butter
- Cover and steam for about 5 minutes or until carrots are tender crisp
- Add cranberries and steam another 1 – 2 minutes
- Place on a serving plate and garnish with the toasted walnuts

4 – 6 servings

Fried Cabbage

2 Tbsp	Vegetable oil
3 cups	Cabbage, finely shredded
1 cup	Apple, chopped
1 small	Onion, chopped
½ tsp	Salt, or to taste
¼ tsp	White pepper

- Heat oil in a large frying pan
- Add cabbage, apple, onion and salt and pepper
- Cook over medium heat about 15 minutes, stirring often
- Cover pan during the last 5 minutes, stirring once or twice
- Vegetables should be tender crisp
- Garnish with parsley

4 servings

Cauliflower Sauté

1 small	Head of cauliflower
1 small	Onion, chopped
1 tsp	Dried dill weed
¼ tsp	White pepper
½ tsp	Salt, or to taste
3 Tbsp	Butter

- Break cauliflower into florets
- Heat butter in a heavy saucepan and add onion
- Stir until the onion is soft
- Add the cauliflower florets, stirring until cauliflower is tender crisp and a nice golden brown
- Add salt and pepper
- Place in a serving dish
- Garnish with dill weed

4 – 6 servings

Fennel and Tomatoes

1 pound	Small fennel roots
2 Tbsp	Water
1 cup	Dry white wine
2 medium	Tomatoes, peeled and quartered
	Salt and pepper to taste
	Dried basil

- Clean fennel thoroughly and cut into quarters
- Cook in 2 Tbsp of water and 3 Tbsp of wine for 5 minutes, stirring often
- If the pan starts to get dry, add a little more wine
- Add tomatoes, the rest of the wine and seasonings
- Cook until fennel is tender crisp, gently stirring occasionally
- Serve on a heated platter garnished with basil

4 – 6 servings

Scalloped Potatoes

1½ pounds	Potatoes
1 can	Cream of mushroom soup
1/3 cup + 2 Tbsp	Water
3 Tbsp	Butter
	Paprika

- Preheat oven to 350°F
- Peel and slice potatoes thinly
- Arrange in a greased 1½ quart oven proof casserole
- Blend soup and water, pour over potatoes
- Dot with butter
- Sprinkle with paprika
- Bake for about 1 hour
- Remove from oven and let stand for about 5 minutes

6 servings

Green Onion Buttered Potatoes

1 ½ pounds	Small new potatoes
2 cups	Chicken broth
¼ tsp	Salt
3 Tbsp	Butter
1 Tbsp	Green onion, chopped – just the green part
3 Tbsp	Cornstarch
1/3 cup	Cold water

- Wash and clean potatoes, leave whole
- Place potatoes in a saucepan
- Add chicken broth, salt and butter
- Just before potatoes are cooked, mix the cornstarch and cold water to make a paste, set aside
- When potatoes are cooked, stir the cornstarch mixture into the saucepan with potatoes and broth
- Stir until thickened
- Place in a serving bowl and garnish with green onions

4 – 6 servings

Fried Spinach

2 Tbsp	Vegetable oil
2 Tbsp	Butter
1 large	Onion, sliced
1¼ pounds	Fresh spinach leaves, washed
	Salt and pepper to taste

- Place vegetable oil and butter in a large heavy saucepan over medium high heat
- Add onion, sauté until lightly browned
- Add spinach, cook tossing constantly for 3 – 5 minutes until wilted and cooked
- Season with salt and pepper

4 servings

BEANS
PASTA
& RICE

Italian Dinner
Homemade Pasta

2 cups	Flour
4 large	Eggs

- Place flour in a large bowl. Make a well in the flour, add eggs and beat eggs into flour with a fork
- When eggs are incorporated into the flour, knead the dough until it is smooth and dry
- Cover the dough and let rest for 25 minutes
- Cut into 4 pieces
- Using one piece at a time, leaving the rest covered, run it through a pasta machine 3 or 4 times at the #1 setting
- If dough is too sticky, brush with flour
- Then run the dough through the pasta machine 3 or 4 times at the #2, #3 and #4 settings
- Run the dough through the pasta cutter for the desired shape
- Lay the pasta on a cloth to dry
- When ready to use, in a large pasta pot bring water, 3 Tbsp salt and 1 Tbsp oil to a rolling boil
- Add the pasta and boil for about 7 minutes or until al dente
- Drain and mix with pasta sauce and top with meatballs

5 – 6 servings

Pasta Sauce

1 – 19 oz can	Tomato sauce
1 medium	Onion, chopped
3 cloves	Garlic, minced
½ tsp	Dried oregano
½ tsp	Dried parsley
1 – 10 oz can	Sliced mushrooms, drained and save liquid
3 Tbsp	Green pepper, chopped
2 Tbsp	Olive oil

- In a large sauce pan, sauté onion, garlic and green pepper in the olive oil until soft
- Add tomato sauce, mushrooms and half the mushroom liquid
- Stir in parsley and oregano, simmer covered for 10 minutes, then add meatballs

Meatballs

1 pound	Ground pork
1 pound	Ground beef
1 medium	Onion, chopped
2 tsp	Salt
¼ tsp	Black pepper
2	Eggs
¼ cup	Parmesan cheese, grated

- Mix ingredients together well, shape into 1½" balls
- Add to pasta sauce and cook covered about 30 min.

Finishing up the meal

- Remove meatballs
- Drain pasta
- Return pasta to pasta pot
- Pour sauce over pasta and toss until well coated
- Place pasta on serving plate
- Top with meatballs
- Serve with parmesan on the side

Serves 5 – 6

Spaghetti and Egg

450 grams	Spaghetti
1 Tbsp	Oil
2 Tbsp	Butter
1 ¼ cups	Half and half
3	Eggs, beaten
1/3 cup	Parmesan cheese, grated
½ tsp	Salt
	Freshly ground black pepper

- Fill a large pot with water, add 2 Tbsp of salt and 1 Tbsp of oil, bring to a boil
- Add spaghetti and cook for approximately 7 minutes, stirring occasionally
- Drain the spaghetti and return to pot
- Add the butter and stir to coat pasta, remove from heat
- Cover pot while preparing egg mixture
- In a bowl, beat the eggs, cream, ½ tsp salt & pepper and parmesan cheese
- Pour over hot spaghetti and toss with 2 forks until spaghetti is evenly coated.
- Return pot to heat and heat until eggs are cooked, tossing constantly with the forks

4 – 6 servings

Pasta with Potatoes

2 cups	Macaroni
2 cups	Potatoes, cubed
2 cups	Frozen peas
1 small	Onion, chopped
2 Tbsp	Olive oil
1 – 14 oz can	Tomato sauce
2 Tbsp	Salt
¼ tsp	Black pepper

- Fill a large pot with water, add salt and bring to a boil
- Add macaroni and potatoes, stir often do not overcook (about 7 – 8 minutes)
- Add the frozen peas and boil 2 minutes
- While pasta is cooking, heat the oil in a small saucepan, add chopped onion, cook until soft
- Add tomato sauce and black pepper and heat through
- Drain macaroni, potatoes and peas then return to the pot, add the tomato sauce
- Toss and serve
- Sprinkle with parmesan cheese

4 – 6 servings

Penne & Vegetables

450 grams	Penne
1 cup	Broccoli florets
1 cup	Asparagus, cut into 1½ - 2" pieces
2 Tbsp	Butter
¼ cup	Beef broth
1 – 14 oz can	Tomato sauce
1/3 cup	Cream
2 Tbsp	Parmesan cheese, grated
2 Tbsp	Salt
1 small	Onion, chopped

- In a small sauce pan, sauté the chopped onion in the butter
- Add the tomato sauce and beef broth, remove from heat and keep warm
- Add penne to a large pot of boiling salted water and cook for about 6 minutes
- Drain the penne reserving all the liquid
- Return liquid to the pot and keep penne warm in a large covered bowl
- Add the broccoli to pasta water cook 2 – 3 minutes
- Add asparagus and cook additional 1 – 2 minutes
- Return penne to pot for an additional minute then drain and return to the pasta pot, keep warm
- Add the cream to the tomato sauce then pour over the drained penne and vegetables and toss gently
- Sprinkle with parmesan cheese

Serves 5 - 6

Macaroni & Cheese

2 cups	Macaroni
2 Tbsp	Butter
2 Tbsp	Flour
1½ cups	Milk
¼ tsp	White pepper
2 cups	Grated sharp cheddar cheese
1	Onion, finely chopped
	Salt to taste

- Preheat oven to 350°F
- Cook macaroni according to package directions
- Drain then rinse in cold water
- Make a white sauce
    - Melt the butter
    - Add the flour, stir well
    - Add milk slowly
    - Stir until the sauce starts to thicken
- Stir in the grated cheese until melted
- Add white pepper
- Pour sauce over the macaroni
- Add the finely chopped onions and stir
- Place mixture in oven proof casserole
- Bake uncovered for 25 minutes

Serves 4 - 6

Chilli Con Carne

2 cups	Onion, chopped
½ cup	Green pepper, chopped
2 pounds	Lean ground beef
4 Tbsp	Fat (butter, margarine or vegetable oil)
2 – 19 oz cans	Red kidney beans, rinsed and drained
1 – 28 oz can	Diced tomatoes
2–4 Tbsp	Chilli powder, or to taste
2 tsp	Salt
½ tsp	Black pepper
2 Tbsp	White vinegar

- Heat the fat in a heavy pot, then brown the onion, green pepper and the ground beef
- Add the kidney beans, diced tomatoes, chilli powder, salt, pepper and vinegar
- Stir well, simmer for 45 minutes – 1 hour, stirring frequently

Serves 8 – 10

Baked Beans

1 pound	White navy beans, dry
¼ pound	Ham, chopped or 1 ham hock
1 large	Onion, chopped
¾ cup	Brown sugar
½ cup	Ketchup
1 tsp	Dry mustard
2 tsp	Salt
2 Tbsp	Worcestershire sauce
1 – 19 oz can	Tomato sauce
1/3 cup	Molasses
1 cup	Boiling water

- In a pot, cover the beans with water and soak overnight, drain in the morning
- Place beans in a large pot and cover with water, bring to a boil for 10 minutes
- Skim off the foam from the water
- Drain beans and transfer to slow cooker or bean pot
- Add remaining ingredients to beans; mix gently
- Bake covered in 350°F oven for 6 – 8 hours or in a slow cooker for 10 hours on high
- Uncover during the last hour, adding more water if beans become dry

Serves 4 – 6

Chinese Dinner

Chow Mien

4 Tbsp	Vegetable oil
1 pound	Boneless pork
1 medium	Onion, chopped – not too fine
3 – 4	Green onions, chopped
5 stalks	Celery, cut into bite sized pieces
1 - 19 oz can	Bean sprouts, drained
1 small package	Chow mien noodles
2 cloves	Garlic, minced
3 Tbsp	Soy sauce
2 Tbsp	Cornstarch
1/3 cup	Cold water
	Sesame seeds

- Preheat oven to 300°F
- Cut pork into bite sized pieces
- Heat vegetable oil in a large skillet then add pork
- While frying, add 1 Tbsp of soy sauce and the minced garlic
- Stir frequently to prevent overcooking
- When the meat is cooked (taste it to be sure) transfer it to an oven proof casserole, leaving the juices in the skillet
- Heat the pan again and add the celery and onions and another Tbsp of oil
- Stir while cooking, about 1 minute
- Remove celery and onions and add to casserole in the oven, leaving the juices in the skillet
- Add the bean sprouts to the skillet and repeat as for the celery and onions.
- Then add sprouts to the casserole in the oven

- Finally, add 2 Tbsp cornstarch mixed in 1/3 cup cold water to the remaining juices in the skillet.
- Add 2 Tbsp soy sauce and cook for about 1 minute
- Place the whole mixture in the oven and cover with the chow mien noodles
- Heat in a 300°F oven and bake for about 20 minutes
- Garnish with green onions

Sweet & Sour Spareribs

1 pound	Small spareribs
2 Tbsp	Flour
3 Tbsp	Soy sauce
2 Tbsp	Shortening
1 clove	Garlic
¼ cup	Rice vinegar
¼ cup	White sugar
½ tsp	Salt
1 small can	Pineapple chunks undrained

- In a large bowl mix the flour, garlic, soy sauce and spareribs together
- Heat shortening in a saucepan until hot, remove spareribs from the bowl and sauté in the hot oil until brown
- Add the rice vinegar, sugar, salt, pineapple and pineapple juice to the skillet, cook for 30 minutes

Fried Rice

1 cup	White rice
1 small	Onion, finely chopped
1 stalk	Celery, finely chopped
1 clove	Garlic, minced
1 tsp	Salt
1 Tbsp	Sesame oil
2 Tbsp	Vegetable oil
2 cups	HOT water

- This recipe requires a large fry pan with a lid
- In the large fry pan place the sesame oil and vegetable oil and heat
- Add the rice and stir until a golden colour appears
- Add the onion, garlic, celery and salt
- Cook another 1 – 2 minutes until the rice is a little darker
- CAREFULLY add the hot water to the fry pan
- Stir and cover
- Lower the heat and cook until the rice is done and the water is absorbed, about 15 - 20 minutes

Serves 4 - 6

BEEF
PORK
& CHICKEN

Beef Stew

2 Tbsp each	Vegetable oil and butter
2 pounds	Lean stewing beef cut into 1 ½" cubes
1½ Tbsp	Flour
2 large	Onions, sliced
1 Tbsp	Salt
½ tsp	Freshly ground pepper
½ tsp	Paprika
1 cup	Red wine
3 cups	Boiling water
1	Bay leaf
¼ tsp	Thyme
2 cups	Rutabagas, cut into chunks
2 cups	Carrots, cut into chunks
4 medium	Potatoes, cut into chunks
2 ribs	Celery, cut into chunks
6 – 8 small	Onions
½ cup	Cold water
¼ cup	Flour

- Place 1 Tbsp of oil in a large bowl, add meat and toss to coat the meat
- In another bowl, mix 1 ½ Tbsp of flour, the salt, pepper and paprika.
- Add this mixture to the meat and toss until meat is coated
- Heat the remaining fat in a stew pot over high heat
- Add the meat and brown well on all sides
- Reduce heat
- Add the sliced onions, cover and cook gently for 5 minutes stirring occasionally
- Add the wine and boiling water, stir to dissolve the caramelized meat juices on the bottom of the pot
- Add thyme and bay leaf.

66

- Cover pot and simmer gently for 1½ - 2 hours or until meat is tender, stirring occasionally
- Add rutabagas and carrots, simmer for 15 minutes
- Add potatoes, onions and celery and simmer for 15 minutes
- Pour cold water into a shaker, add ¼ cup flour then shake to blend
- Remove stew from heat, stir in the flour mixture
- Return to heat and cook gently for 5 minutes, stirring constantly until gravy thickens

Serves 6

Meat Loaf

1 ½ pounds	Lean ground beef
1 cup	Cracker crumbs
2	Eggs, beaten
1 cup	Tomato sauce
½ cup	Onion, finely chopped
2 Tbsp	Green pepper, finely chopped
2 Tbsp	Red pepper, finely chopped
1 tsp	Salt
¼ tsp	Ground black pepper
	Chilli sauce

- Preheat oven to 350°F
- In a large bowl, combine all ingredients except the chilli sauce
- Mix well then shape mixture into a loaf pan
- Score the loaf by pressing with the handle of a wooden spoon
- Fill the score marks with the chilli sauce
- Bake for one hour

Serves 6

Chicken Dijon

4	Chicken breasts, boneless
2	Eggs
3 1/3 Tbsp	Dijon mustard
2/3 cup	Bread crumbs
1/4 tsp	Garlic powder
1/4 tsp	Onion powder
1/4 tsp	Dried thyme
1/2 cup	Flour
1/3 cup	Cream
1 Tbsp	Sugar
4 tsp	Minced fresh parsley

- Preheat oven to 400°F
- Rinse chicken with cold water and pat dry
- In a shallow bowl or pie plate, blend eggs and 2 Tbsp of Dijon mustard
- In another plate, place bread crumbs
- Place flour, garlic powder, onion powder and Thyme on another plate
- Coat chicken with flour mixture
- Dip chicken in egg/mustard mixture
- Roll in bread crumbs to coat
- Bake for 20 minutes or until done
- In a small bowl blend the remaining mustard, cream and sugar
- Drizzle over cooked chicken and sprinkle with parsley

Serves 4

Pork Chops with Apricots

3 Tbsp	Butter
4	Pork chops, ¾ - 1 inch thick
3 Tbsp	Vegetable oil
1	Onion, chopped
2 cloves	Garlic, minced
½ tsp	Salt
1/8 tsp	Pepper
½ cup	Orange juice
2 cups	Water
12	Dried apricots

- Preheat oven to 350°F
- Melt butter in oven proof pan, brown pork chops for about 3 minutes on each side, remove pork chops, cover and set aside
- Add onion to the pan and cook until transparent
- Return pork chops to pan, add garlic and apricots
- Add salt, pepper, orange juice and water
- Cover & bake in the oven for 45 minutes
- Reduce the heat to 325°F
- Remove the cover and bake for 30 minutes longer

Serves 4

Corned Beef and Cabbage

5 – 6 pounds	Corned brisket
1 tsp	White vinegar
1 tsp	Sugar
1 small – medium	Cabbage, cut into wedges
8 medium	Carrots, peeled, cut into 2" pieces
8 medium	Potatoes, peeled, cut into 2" pieces

- Rinse the brine from the brisket
- Add to a large pot then cover with cold water and bring to a boil
- Add the vinegar and sugar then simmer for 4 hours or until a fork won't stick in the thickest part of the brisket
- Add the carrots and potatoes and cook until they're almost done
- Add the cabbage and cook until it's cooked
- Remove vegetables and meat from the pot; slice meat onto a serving plate and place vegetables around it

Serves 5 - 6

Devilled Chicken

3 pounds	Chicken (breasts or thighs)
2 Tbsp	Vegetable oil or butter
½ tsp	Salt
¼ tsp	White pepper

- Preheat oven to 350°F
- Line a shallow oven proof pan with foil
- Brush chicken with oil
- Sprinkle lightly with salt and pepper
- Cover loosely with foil (do not seal)
- Bake for 1½ hours or until chicken is tender
- Lower oven to 200°F
- Cover tightly with the foil and keep warm in oven

Devilled Sauce

2 small	Onions, chopped fine
2 large	Garlic clove, crushed
2 cups	Chicken broth
1/8 tsp	White pepper
3 Tbsp	Butter
3 Tbsp	Flour
¼ tsp	Curry powder
1 Tbsp	Water
¼ tsp	Worcestershire sauce
1 Tbsp	Chilli sauce

- Place onion, pepper, garlic and 2 cups chicken stock in a small sauce pan and simmer for 20 minutes
- Strain the stock and return liquid to measuring cup
- Measure the stock then add enough chicken broth to make 2 cups of liquid

72

- Melt the butter in a sauce pan
- Blend in the flour
- Add stock gradually, stirring until thick and smooth
- Combine curry powder and water to make a paste
- Add curry paste, chilli sauce and Worcestershire sauce to the flour and chicken stock mixture, stir until thick and smooth
- Serve the sauce over the chicken and garnish with parsley

Serves 6

Variation: Recipe can also be made with pork chops or pork tenderloin instead of chicken

Apricot Glazed Cornish Game Hens

| 6 - 1–1½ lb | Game hens, washed and dried |
| ½ - 2/3 cups | Apricot jam, melted |

- Salt inside and outside of hens
- Stuff with wild rice pilaff (see next recipe)
- Place each hen on a rack in a roasting pan, rub each hen with butter
- Roast for 55 – 65 minutes in 425°F oven
- After 25 minutes, baste hens with melted apricot jam continue roasting; baste every 15 minutes until done
- Remove from the oven and place a tent of foil over the hens and let rest 15 – 20 minutes
- Place on serving tray and garnish with parsley and apricot halves (if fresh apricots are not available, use dried)

Serves 6

Rice Pilaf

1 cup	Rice
3 cups	Chicken broth
½ tsp	Salt
2 Tbsp	Butter
½ cup	Onions, finely chopped
½ cup	Celery, chopped
¼ cup	Green pepper, chopped
¼ cup	Red pepper chopped
½ tsp	Salt
1/8 tsp	Freshly ground pepper

- Melt butter in a saucepan
- Add onion, celery, green and red peppers cook until tender, stirring frequently
- Add rice and stir until mixed
- Add chicken broth, salt and pepper
- Cook covered over low heat 20 minutes or until rice is done
- Stuff lightly into game hens

Serves 6

Stuffed Pork Tenderloin

3	Pork tenderloin; 11 – 12 " long
12 – 15	Dried prunes
1 Tbsp	Oil
2 Tbsp	Butter
	Salt and pepper to taste

- Cut about an inch off of each end of the tenderloins to make three even cylinder shapes
- Save the cut off pieces for another meal
- Insert a knife sharpening steel lengthwise down the centre of each tenderloin, remove the steel
- Insert 4 – 5 prunes into each tenderloin
- Melt butter and oil in a large oven safe pan, add stuffed tenderloins and brown on all sides over medium high heat
- Place the pan in a preheated 350°F oven for 30 – 35 minutes, or until meat is done
- Remove meat from oven and place on a plate and let rest covered with foil
- Add flour to drippings in the pan then slowly add 1-cup water. Stir until gravy is smooth
- Cut the tenderloin into 1½" medallions
- Place medallions on a serving tray, spoon gravy around and garnish with parsley and a few prunes

Serves 6 - 8

Oven Barbecued Ribs

5 pounds	Spareribs
1 large	Onion
2	Bay leaves
1 tsp	Chopped garlic
1 tsp	Pickling spice
1 Tbsp	Salt
¾ - 1 cup	Barbecue sauce
¼ - ½ cup	Honey or syrup

- In a large stock pot, place spareribs, onion, bay leaves, garlic salt and spices
- Cover with water and bring to a boil
- Lower heat and simmer 30 – 40 minutes
- Remove ribs and place on a baking sheet
- Mix barbecue sauce and honey or syrup together
- With a pastry brush, brush sauce over the spareribs
- Place in a 400°F oven
- Bake for 45 minutes to an hour, turning and basting every 7 to 10 minutes
- Check frequently to ensure the sauce isn't burning

Serves 4 - 5

SEAFOOD

Curried Prawns

2 Tbsp	Butter
4 Tbsp	Flour
1 small	Onion, chopped
1 clove	Garlic, minced
2 cups	Milk
3 – 4 Tbsp	Curry powder
½ tsp	Salt
¼ tsp	Black pepper
1½ cups	Frozen peas
½ pound	Prawns, size 31 – 40 per pound; cooked and frozen

- Melt butter, sauté onion and garlic for 1½ - 2 minutes
- Add flour, stir well
- Gradually add milk and when sauce starts to thicken and becomes smooth, add the curry powder, salt and pepper stirring until the sauce becomes smooth again
- Add frozen peas, cook 4 minutes
- Add prawns, heat through, about 4 – 5 minutes
- To serve, ladle over cooked rice

Serves 4

Cod with Sunflower Seeds

2 Tbsp	Butter
1 Tbsp	Dried parsley
1 Tbsp	Dried chives
2 cups	Sunflower seeds, coarsely chopped
4	Cod fillets, skinned
2 Tbsp	Oil
	Salt and pepper

- Preheat oven to 400°F
- In a small pot, melt the 2 Tbsp of butter
- Add dried parsley, dried chives and sunflower seeds
- Add salt and pepper to taste
- Press ¼ of the mixture on top of each fillet
- Place on a baking pan
- Drizzle the oil over each fillet
- Bake for 15 minutes or until the fish flesh is firm and the seeds are golden
- Garnish with parsley and grapes

Serves 4

Smoked Cod and Sauce

4, 6-oz pieces	Smoked cod
4 Tbsp	Butter
4 Tbsp	Flour
2 cups	Milk
¼ cup	Onion, finely chopped
1/8 tsp each	Salt and pepper

- Melt butter in a sauce pan and add finely chopped onion
- Stir to soften
- Stir in flour, salt and pepper
- When well mixed, add milk slowly, stirring until smooth and slightly thickened
- Add cod and simmer (do not boil) for about 10 – 15 minutes
- When done, place in a shallow serving dish and garnish with fresh parsley

Serves 4

Sole Baked with Lemon

4, 6-oz	Sole fillets
1	Leek, chopped (white part only)
2 cloves	Garlic, minced
½ tsp	Dried thyme
¼ tsp	Salt
¼ tsp	White pepper
1	Lemon – juice plus the grated rind
2 Tbsp	Cooking oil

- Preheat oven to 350°F
- Lay the fillets in an oven proof casserole
- Sprinkle the leek, garlic and thyme on top
- Season with salt and pepper
- Mix lemon juice and oil together, drizzle over the fish
- Bake for about 15 minutes
- Transfer to a serving dish, sprinkle top with lemon rind
- Garnish with lemon wedges and parsley

Serves 4

Halibut with Blueberry Sauce

2 pounds	Halibut fillets
2 Tbsp	Butter
	Salt and pepper to taste
2 ½ cups	Blueberries, mashed
1 Tbsp	Cornstarch
2 tsp	Lemon juice
1 Tbsp	Sherry

- Cut halibut into serving-sized portions
- Salt and pepper both sides of each piece
- Grease a fry pan lightly with butter
- Brown halibut slightly on each side (5 minutes per inch of thickness)
- Remove from skillet and keep warm while making sauce
- Combine blueberries, cornstarch and lemon juice
- Heat until cooked and the sauce is slightly thickened
- Add sherry and cook one minute longer
- Spoon around the halibut and garnish with lemon wedges

Serves 4 - 6

Salmon Casserole

1 – 10 oz can	Cream of mushroom soup
1 – 7 oz can	Salmon, drained
2 cups	Cooked macaroni
1 cup	Frozen peas
1 – 10 oz can	Sliced mushrooms, drained
	Salt to taste
1 cup	Bread crumbs

- Preheat oven to 375°F
- In an oven proof casserole, layer the ingredients as follows:
    - Add the macaroni
    - 1/3 of the cream of mushroom soup
    - Add the salmon
    - 1/3 of the cream of mushroom soup
    - The frozen peas and sliced mushrooms
    - Remaining 1/3 of the soup
- Sprinkle bread crumbs on top
- Bake for 30 minutes

4 – 1-cup servings

Tuna Casserole

1 cup	Macaroni
2 cans	Solid tuna, drained and rinsed
¼ cup	Melted butter
2 Tbsp	Onion, chopped
2 Tbsp	Red pepper, chopped
¼ cup	Flour
2 cups	Milk
½ tsp	Worcestershire sauce
1 ½ cups	Grated cheddar cheese

- Preheat oven to 350°F
- Boil macaroni in salted water until tender
- Drain, and place in greased 2-quart casserole
- Add tuna and mix gently
- Melt butter in a saucepan, add onion and peppers, cook until the onion is golden
- Blend in the flour
- Gradually add the milk and cook until sauce is thick and smooth
- Add salt and pepper to taste
- Add Worcestershire sauce
- Stir in grated cheese
- Pour this sauce over the tuna and macaroni
- Bake for 25 minutes

Serves 4 – 5

Salmon Loaf

1 – 14 oz can	Salmon, drained, skin and bones removed
1 cup	Crackers, crushed
½ cup	Red pepper, finely chopped
½ cup	Onion, finely chopped
1 – 10 oz can	Creamed corn
1	Egg
¼ tsp	Salt
¼ tsp	White pepper

- Preheat oven to 350°F
- In medium bowl, combine all ingredients together and mix well
- Shape into a loaf and place in a greased loaf pan
- Bake 30 – 35 minutes
- Remove from oven and let sit for a few minutes
- Turn out onto a serving plate
- Garnish with lemon wedges

Serves 4 – 6

BREAD
& BUNS

Brown Bread

2 cups	Cold water
1/3 cup	Corn meal
½ cup	Molasses
1/3 cup	Brown sugar
1 Tbsp	Salt
1/3 cup	Shortening
½ cup	Warm water
2 Tbsp	Dry yeast
1 cup	Whole wheat flour
6 – 8 cups	All purpose flour

- Put corn meal and cold water in sauce pan and bring to a boil, cook for 3 minutes (the reason for starting in cold water is to stir the lumps out)
- Put the next 4 ingredients in a mixing bowl
- Pour corn meal over to melt shortening
- Add 1½ cups more water so the mixture will be lukewarm
- Meanwhile, soak yeast in the ½ cup of lukewarm water to which ½ tsp of sugar has been added, let stand 10 minutes
- Add to the mixture in the bowl
- Add whole wheat flour and enough white flour to make a soft dough
- Turn on a lightly floured surface
- Knead until smooth, about 10 minutes adding more flour as required
- Place dough into a large greased bowl
- Cover and let rise about 1 – 1½ hours
- Punch dough down, turn out onto a board and divide into three pieces
- Shape each piece and place into a greased loaf pan
- Cover and let stand until double in size, about 45 minutes

- Preheat oven to 350°F and bake 35 – 40 minutes
- Brush tops of loaves with melted butter if desired
- Cool

Yield 3 loaves

Overnight Buns

1 packet	Yeast
½ cup	Warm water
¼ cup	Sugar
2 cups	Warm water
½ cup	Oil
1	Egg, beaten
1 tsp	Salt
½ cup	Sugar
7 – 8 cups	Flour

- Combine the ¼ cup sugar and ½ cup water then stir in the yeast, let set for 5 minutes, whip with a fork
- In a large bowl, put 2 cups warm water, ½ cup oil, egg, salt, sugar and yeast mixture
- Add 7 – 8 cups of flour, ¼ at a time
- Mix together and knead until smooth
- Place dough into a greased bowl
- Let rise for 45 minutes to an hour
- Punch down, cover and let stand for an hour; punch down again
- Shape into rolls and place onto a baking sheet; cover and leave overnight
- In the morning, bake in a 375°F oven for 15 – 20 minutes

Yield 10 – 12 buns

Irish Soda Bread

2 cups	All purpose flour
2 cups	Whole wheat flour
2 Tbsp	Brown sugar
2 tsp	Baking powder
1 tsp	Baking soda
1 tsp	Salt
2 cups	Buttermilk
1	Egg, beaten
$\frac{1}{4}$ cup	Oatmeal

- Preheat oven to 375°F
- Combine flour, brown sugar, baking powder, baking soda and salt in a mixing bowl. Stir well to blend
- Mix buttermilk and egg and add to flour mixture
- Stir until all ingredients are moistened
- Dust a board with oatmeal and knead dough 10 to 12 times to coat the dough with oats, form into a round ball
- Cut a cross lightly on top of loaf
- Placed on a greased baking sheet
- Bake for 45 – 50 minutes or until the bread sounds hollow
- Serve warm

Yield 1 loaf

Coffee Buns

4 cups	All purpose flour
1 cup	White sugar
1 cup	Cold butter
1 tsp	Baking soda
2 tsp	Cream of tartar
1 tsp	Salt
1	Egg, beaten
	Milk

- Preheat oven to 375°F
- Sift dry ingredients together
- Cut in butter as if you are making pastry
- Add well beaten egg plus enough milk to make a soft dough
- Roll out dough on a lightly floured board to ½ inch thick
- Make filling
  - 1 egg beaten
  - 1 cup brown sugar
  - 1 cup coconut
- Combine filling ingredients; spread on the rolled out dough
- Roll up jelly roll fashion; cut into ¾" slices
- Placed on greased baking pan
- Bake 15 – 20 minutes

Yield 8 – 10 buns

Light Airy Buns

1 packet	Yeast
¼ cup	Luke warm water
1 tsp	Sugar
2 cups	Milk, scalded
½ cup	Butter
1 ½ Tbsp	Sugar
1 ½ tsp	Salt
2	Eggs, well beaten
4 cups	Flour

- Combine yeast, lukewarm water and sugar, let stand 10 minutes
- Put butter, sugar, salt and hot milk in large mixer bowl and stir until butter is melted
- When the yeast has risen, add to the lukewarm milk mixture, stir well and add beaten eggs & flour
- Beat with the mixer thoroughly (it's important to use an electric mixer at this point to develop a vigorous beating as there is no kneading done to develop the gluten) then return to a greased bowl
- Cover and let rise in a warm place until doubled, 1 ½ hours, then beat dough again with the mixer
- Set oven to 425°F
- Place by spoonfuls into greased muffin tins, let rise again, about 30 minutes
- Bake in hot oven for 10 to 15 minutes

Yield 8 – 10 buns

Fried Bread

1 packet	Yeast
1 tsp	Sugar
½ cup	Warm water
¼ cup each	Lard and butter
1 Tbsp	Salt
3 Tbsp	White sugar
½ cup	Powdered milk
2 cups each	Boiling water and cold water
6	Eggs, beaten
6 – 8 cups	Flour

- Dissolve yeast and sugar in the warm water, let stand for 10 minutes
- Combine lard, butter, salt, sugar and powdered milk in a large bowl, add 2 cups boiling water and stir until all is dissolved
- Add 2 cups cold water then the yeast mixture
- Add 2 cups flour to make a soft batter
- Add 6 beaten eggs, 4 – 6 cups flour & knead until smooth
- Let rise once, about 1 hour,
- Punch down and rise again about 45 minutes or until doubled
- Cut into pieces and roll into long fingers.
- Press 3 fingers together at one end then braid together
- Place on a baking pan and let rise again, about 45 minutes or until doubled
- While waiting for them to rise, place 3 cups of vegetable oil in a saucepan and bring to 350°F over medium heat.
- When braids have risen, fry on both sides until golden
- Drain on paper towel
- Store in a covered container

Scones

1 cup	Brown sugar
1/3 cup	Shortening
1	Egg
2 cups	All purpose flour
2 tsp	Baking powder
½ tsp	Baking soda
1/3 cup	Milk
½ cup	Raisins

- Preheat oven to 350°F
- Cream shortening and sugar, add egg and beat until light
- Mix dry ingredients together add to shortening, egg and sugar mixture alternately with the milk
- Fold in the raisins
- Drop by Tbsp onto a greased baking pan
- Bake 10 – 15 minutes

Yield 8 – 12

MUFFINS
& LOAVES

Bran Muffins

2 cups	All bran
3 cups	White sugar
3 Tbsp	Baking soda
2 tsp	Salt
4	Eggs
2 cups	Boiling water
1 cup	Margarine or butter
2 cups	Raisins
2 cups	Bran flakes
3 cups	Buttermilk
2 Tbsp	Molasses
5 cups	All purpose flour

- Pour boiling water over all bran, cool
- Cream margarine and sugar, add eggs and beat well
- Add cooled all bran, dry ingredients and the buttermilk
- Add raisins and fold in the bran flakes
- Do not use the first day
- Refrigerate in air tight container
- Batter will be good for 3 weeks
- Fill lined muffin tins ¾ full
- Bake 15 – 20 minutes in a 375°F oven

Yield approx 4 dozen

Oatmeal Muffins

1 ¼ cups	All purpose flour
1 cup	Rolled oats
¼ cup	Brown sugar
3 tsp	Baking powder
½ tsp	Salt
¼ tsp	Cinnamon
¾ cup	Raisins
1	Egg
2 Tbsp	Molasses
¼ cup	Vegetable oil
1 cup	Milk
1 tsp	Vanilla

- Preheat oven to 400°F
- Place flour, rolled oats, brown sugar, baking powder, salt, cinnamon and raisins in a large bowl; mix together
- Beat eggs in a small bowl until frothy
- Mix in molasses, vegetable oil, milk and vanilla
- Pour liquids over dry ingredients and stir just to moisten; batter will be lumpy
- Fill greased muffin cups ¾ full
- Bake for 20 – 25 minutes

Yield 1 dozen

Biscuits

2 cups	All purpose flour
1 Tbsp	Baking powder
½ tsp	Salt
¼ cup	Cold butter
¾ cup	Sour cream
¼ cup	Milk
¼ tsp	Baking soda

- Preheat oven to 375°F
- In a mixing bowl add flour, baking powder, salt and baking soda
- Cut butter into the flour mixture until it looks like crumbs
- Blend in sour cream
- Stir in milk until moist
- Gather the dough together and on a lightly floured board, roll out and cut into rounds with a cookie cutter or a glass
- Place biscuits on baking pan and bake for 15 minutes

Yield 10 - 12

Carrot Muffins

1 cup	Whole wheat flour
1 cup	All purpose flour
1 Tbsp	Baking powder
½ tsp	Salt
¼ cup	Brown sugar
½ tsp	Cinnamon
1 cup	Coarsely grated carrots
1 tsp	Grated orange rind
1 cup	Milk
¼ cup	Melted butter
¼ cup	Molasses
¾ cup	Raisins

- Preheat oven to 400°F
- Mix flour, baking powder, salt, sugar and cinnamon
- Stir in carrots and orange rind
- Combine milk, melted butter and molasses
- Add to dry ingredients all at once, stirring just to moisten
- Fold in raisins
- Fill greased muffin tins ¾ full
- Bake about 25 minutes or until golden brown

Yield 1 dozen

Baking Powder Biscuits

2 cups	All purpose flour
½ tsp	Salt
3 tsp	Baking powder
¾ cup	Milk
6 Tbsp	Shortening

- Preheat oven to 450°F
- Sift flour with salt and baking powder
- Cut in the shortening until the mixture resembles coarse crumbs
- Add milk all at once and stir quickly, just until mixed
- Turn out onto a lightly floured board and knead lightly for about one minute or just enough to form the dough into a smooth ball
- Pat out to ½" thick and cut with a floured biscuit cutter
- Place biscuits on an ungreased baking sheet
- Bake for 12 – 15 minutes

Yield 10 – 12

Date Loaf

1 cup	Sugar
1 cup	Dates
1 tsp	Baking soda
1 cup	Boiling water
2	Eggs, beaten
1 ½ cups	All purpose flour
¼ tsp	Salt
1 ½ tsp	Allspice
3 Tbsp	Butter
½ cup	Chopped walnuts (optional)

- Preheat oven to 350°F
- Cut dates, sprinkle with baking soda and cover with boiling water, stir and cool
- Add butter, sugar and eggs to cooled dates
- Add flour, allspice, salt and optional walnuts, mix well
- Pour into a greased loaf pan
- Bake for 1 hour or until done

Yield 1 loaf

Orange Date Loaf

½ cup	Margarine
¾ cup	White sugar
1	Egg, beaten
Rind	From one orange
½ cup	Orange juice
1 cup	Flour
½ cup	Whole wheat flour
1 tsp	Baking powder
1 tsp	Baking soda
½ tsp	Salt
½ cup	Dates, chopped

- Preheat oven to 350°F
- Cream butter and sugar together
- Add beaten egg and mix well
- Add orange rind
- Sift flours, salt, baking powder and baking soda together and add chopped dates
- Combine butter, sugar & egg with the dry ingredients and the orange juice
- Stir just until blended and put into a greased and floured loaf pan
- Bake for 40 – 50 minutes

Yield 1 loaf

Zucchini Nut Loaf

2	Eggs
2 cups	Grated zucchini
3 cups	All purpose flour
¼ tsp	Ground ginger
¼ tsp	Nutmeg
3 tsp	Cinnamon
1 cup	Chopped walnuts
2 cups	Sugar
3 tsp	Vanilla
1 cup	Vegetable oil
1 tsp	Baking soda
½ tsp	Baking powder
1 tsp	Salt

- Preheat oven to 325°F
- Beat eggs until fluffy
- Blend in sugar, zucchini, salad oil and vanilla
- Add dry ingredients to the egg-sugar mixture
- Stir in the nuts
- Put into two greased and floured loaf pans
- Bake for one hour

Yield 1 loaf

Orange Cranberry Loaf

2 cups	All purpose flour
1 tsp	Salt
1 ½ tsp	Baking powder
½ tsp	Baking soda
1 cup	Sugar
2 Tbsp	Melted butter
	Boiling water
1	Egg, beaten
1 cup	Raw cranberries, rough chopped
1 cup	Chopped walnuts
1	Orange, the rind and the juice

- Preheat oven to 350°F
- To the juice and rind, add melted butter and enough boiling water to make ¾ cup, cool
- Add one beaten egg
- Then add dry ingredients
- Add 1 cup of chopped walnuts and the cranberries; mix together
- Place in a greased and floured loaf pan
- Bake for one hour

Yield 1 loaf

CAKES

Jelly Roll

¾ cup	Cake flour
¾ tsp	Baking powder
4	Eggs
¾ cup	Sugar
1 tsp	Vanilla
¼ tsp	Salt
	Jelly

- Preheat oven to 400°F
- Combine baking powder, salt and eggs in a bowl
- Place this bowl over a smaller bowl of hot water and beat with a beater
- Add sugar gradually
- Remove the bowl from the water
- Add flour and vanilla
- Bake for 13 minutes in a jelly roll pan lined with waxed paper
- When done, turn out onto a tea towel sprinkled with icing sugar
- Spread with jelly and roll up
- Wrap in the tea towel to hold shape
- Let cool then slice into ½" - ¾" slices

Yield approx 12 – 18 slices

Carrot Cake

2 cups	All purpose flour, sifted
1 tsp	Baking powder
1 tsp	Baking soda
1 tsp	Cinnamon
½ tsp	Salt
1 ½ cups	Vegetable oil
2 cup	Sugar
4	Eggs
2 cups	Finely ground carrots
½ cup	Finely chopped pecans

- Preheat oven to 350°F
- Sift together flour, baking powder, baking soda, cinnamon and salt, set aside
- Combine the vegetable oil and sugar, mix well
- Add 4 eggs one at a time beating well after each addition
- Gradually add dry ingredients, mixing well
- Add finely ground carrots and the nuts, mix well
- Bake in greased and floured pan, 50 – 60 minutes

Frosting:
Beat ½ cup butter and 8 ounces cream cheese together until light and fluffy. While still beating, gradually add 2 cups sifted icing sugar. Then add 1 tsp of vanilla and 1 cup finely chopped pecans. Spread over the cooled cake

Cupcakes

2/3 cup	Shortening
2 cups	White sugar
1 tsp	Vanilla
3 cups	Sifted flour
¼ tsp	Salt
3 tsp	Baking powder
1 cup	Milk
3	Eggs

- Preheat oven to 375°F
- Cream shortening, sugar and vanilla
- Add eggs and beat well
- Add sifted flour and baking powder alternately with milk
- Fill lined muffin tins ¾ full
- Bake 10 – 15 minutes

Yield 1 dozen

Crumb Cake

2 cups	All purpose flour
2 cup	Brown sugar
¾ cup	Margarine
1 cup	Sour milk
1 tsp	Baking soda
1 tsp	Cloves
1 tsp	Cinnamon
1	Egg beaten
1 cup	Raisins
¼ tsp	Salt

- Preheat oven to 375°F
- Combine flour, brown sugar and margarine and mix together to form a crumb like mixture, set aside 1 cup of this mixture for the topping
- Add cloves, cinnamon and salt to the remaining crumb mixture and make a well in the centre
- Combine the baking soda, the sour milk and the beaten egg and pour into well in crumb mixture; add raisins and mix well
- Pour into a greased 8" x 8" cake pan and sprinkle with reserved crumb mixture
- Bake for 35 – 40 minutes

Note: to make sour milk, replace 1 Tbsp of fresh milk with 1 Tbsp of lemon juice or white vinegar

Banana Cake

1/3 cup	Shortening
¾ cup	Brown sugar
¾ tsp	Vanilla
1	Egg, well beaten
¾ cup	Mashed bananas
1 ½ cups	Sifted cake flour
1 tsp	Baking powder
½ tsp	Salt
½ tsp	Baking soda
2 Tbsp	Thick sour milk

- Preheat oven to 375°F
- Cream together shortening, sugar and vanilla, beat until light, add egg and mashed bananas
- Add sifted dry ingredients alternately with sour milk beating quickly and lightly until smooth
- Pour into two 8" x 8" cake pans or one 9" x 13" pan
- Bake for 35 – 40 minutes or until done in centre
- Cool for 15 minutes before removing from pan

Note: to make sour milk, replace 1 tsp of fresh milk with 1 tsp of lemon juice or white vinegar

Frosting:
Melt ½ cup butter in saucepan, add 1 cup packed brown sugar and boil over heat stirring constantly. Add ¼ cup of milk and stir until mixture boils. Remove from heat and cool to lukewarm. Add 1¾ - 2 cups of icing sugar and beat until fluffy enough to frost the cake.

Fruit Platz

½ cup	Margarine
1 cup	Sugar
2	Eggs, well beaten
2 cups	All purpose flour
¾ cup	Milk
1 tsp	Vanilla
2 tsp	Baking powder
	Prune plums, halved

- Preheat oven to 375°F
- Cream margarine, sugar & vanilla, beat well and add eggs
- Add flour and baking powder alternately with milk
- Place in a greased 13" x 9" baking pan
- Place fruit over the batter, covering completely
- Sprinkle the crumb topping over the fruit
- Bake for 30 – 35 minutes

Crumb topping:
Combine 1 cup white sugar, ¾ cup margarine and 2 cups of flour in a bowl. Rub together until it forms a crumb-like mixture

Chocolate Cake

2 cups	Sugar
1 cup	Margarine, softened
1 tsp	Vanilla
2	Eggs
2½ cups	Cake flour
1 cup	Cocoa
2 tsp	Baking soda
½ tsp	Salt
2¼ cups	Buttermilk

- Preheat oven to 350°F
- Grease and flour three 9" round baking pans
- Beat sugar, margarine and vanilla in a large bowl with an electric mixer on medium speed until light and fluffy then beat in eggs one at a time
- Combine flour, cocoa, baking soda and salt and add to the sugar mixture alternately with the buttermilk, beat for one minute longer
- Pour into pans and bake for 30 – 35 minutes or until a tester comes out dry
- Cool 10 minutes then remove from pan to wire rack and cool completely before frosting

Frosting:
Combine 6 cups icing sugar, 1 cup softened butter or margarine, 4 – 6 Tbsp milk, 1½ tsp vanilla and beat at medium speed until light and fluffy. Spread on cooled cake

Walnut Torte

8 large	Eggs
8 Tbsp	White sugar
4 Tbsp	Ground walnuts
4 Tbsp	Sifted flour
½ tsp	Baking powder

- Preheat oven to 375°F
- Beat eggs really well (7 – 10 minutes) until thick enough to stand on a spoon
- Add sugar 1 Tbsp at a time, mixing after each addition
- Beat another 3 – 5 minutes
- Combine the sifted flour with baking powder then sift again
- Gently stir ground walnuts into the flour mixture.
- Fold into egg-sugar mixture 1 Tbsp at a time
- Do not over mix
- Bake for 35 – 40 minutes in a large greased and floured spring form pan

Beet Cake

1¾ cups	Flour
1½ cups	Sugar
1½ tsp	Baking soda
½ tsp	Salt
6 Tbsp	Cocoa
1 cup	Vegetable oil (minus 1 Tbsp)
1 tsp	Vanilla
4	Eggs
1½ cups	Grated cooked beets

- Preheat oven to 350°F
- Beat eggs, sugar and vanilla until well mixed and light; add the oil and beat well
- Add flour, baking soda, salt and cocoa and mix well; add the beets
- Bake in greased and floured 9" x 13" pan, 50 minutes

Frosting:
Beat ½ cup butter and 8 ounces cream cheese together until light and fluffy. While still beating, gradually add 2 cups sifted icing sugar. Then add 1 tsp of vanilla. Spread over the cooled cake

Sponge Cake

5 large	Eggs
1 ½ cups	Sugar
1 ½ cups	Flour
½ tsp	Cream of tartar
1/8 tsp	Salt
½ tsp	Vanilla

- Preheat oven to 350°F
- Measure and sift flour, set aside
- Separate the eggs
- Beat the whites into a stiff froth
- Add sugar slowly
- Add cream of tartar
- Then add the salt
- Beat the egg yolks together until thick
- Fold the egg white mixture to egg yolks
- Add the flour slowly folding gently after each addition
- Fold in vanilla
- Bake in an ungreased tube pan for 35 – 45 minutes
- Cool cake on wire rack before removing from pan
- Serve with whipped cream and fruit or topped with your favourite frosting

Lemon Cake

1 cup	Butter
2 cups	Brown sugar
4	Eggs
3½ cups	Flour
2 cups	Raisins
1½ tsp	Baking soda
Rind	2 lemons
1½ cups	Sour milk

- Preheat oven to 350°F
- Cream butter and sugar until well mixed
- Add eggs and lemon rind and beat until fluffy
- Add raisins that have been lightly coated with flour
- Add remaining flour alternately with the sour milk and baking soda
- Place in a greased and floured 9" x 9" pan
- Bake 45 minutes
- While still hot, top with a mixture of the juice of 2 lemons and ¾ cup of brown sugar

Christmas Nut Roll

4 cups	Flour
1 tsp	Salt
1 tsp	Baking powder
1	Egg, slightly beaten
½ pound	Shortening
1/3 cup	Cold water
2Tbsp	Oil

- Preheat oven to 275°F
- Mix all dry ingredients together
- Cut in the shortening
- Combine the egg, cold water and oil, add to the flour shortening mixture
- Knead the dough and let rest covered for about 2 hours
- Roll out very, very thinly
- Spread with the following filling; mix together:
    - ¾ cup brown sugar
    - 1 Tbsp cinnamon
    - ¾ cup coarsely chopped filberts
    - ¾ cup raisins
- Roll up jelly roll fashion, sealing the ends
- Place on a baking sheet
- Bake for about 1 hour

Spice Cake

½ cup	Butter or margarine
2 cups	Brown sugar
3 eggs	Separated
2 cups	Flour, sifted
¼ tsp	Salt
1 tsp	Baking soda
1 tsp	Cinnamon
1 tsp	Cloves
¼ tsp	Nutmeg
1 cup	Sour cream

- Preheat oven to 350°F
- Cream butter or margarine together until fluffy
- Add beaten egg yolks
- Sift dry ingredients together three times and add alternately with sour cream to the shortening/sugar mixture, beating well after each addition
- Fold in stiffly beaten egg whites
- Pour into 9" x 9" cake pan lined with waxed paper
- Bake for 45 - 50 minutes

Seven Minute icing
- Combine the following in the top of double boiler: 1 egg white unbeaten, 7/8 cups white sugar, 3 Tbsp cold water, ½ tsp vanilla
- Place over boiling water and beat for 7 minutes

Spread quickly over cake

Matrimonial Cake

1 ¼ cups	Oatmeal
1 ¼ cups	All purpose flour
½ cup	Brown sugar
1 tsp	Baking soda
¾ cup	Butter

- Preheat oven to 350°F
- Prepare date paste then set aside to cool (see below)
- Sift and measure flour, add soda then sift again
- Cream butter and sugar
- Add oatmeal and flour mixture and mix until crumbly texture
- Grease an 8" x 8" pan, press about ½ of the mixture into the bottom of the pan
- Spread on cooled date paste
- Put remaining crumb mixture on top, press down gently
- Bake for about 30 minutes

Date Paste
- 2 cups dates, washed, stoned and cut into pieces
- 1 cup boiling water
- 1 Tbsp brown sugar
- 1 Tbsp lemon juice
- Cook dates and brown sugar in boiling water stirring frequently until smooth. Add lemon juice then set aside to cool

Unbaked Cheesecake

Base

1 cup	Graham wafer crumbs
¼ cup	Sugar
¼ cup	Melted butter

- Combine graham wafer crumbs, sugar and melted butter; press on to bottom of 9-inch spring form pan

Filling

1 envelope	Unflavoured gelatine
¼ cup	Cold water
1 - 8 oz pkg	Cream cheese, softened
½ cup	White sugar
¾ cup	Milk
¼ cup	Lemon juice
1 cup	Whipping cream, whipped
	Strawberries for garnish

- Soften gelatine in water, stirring over low heat until dissolved
- Combine cream cheese and sugar, mix at medium speed until well blended
- While still mixing, gradually add gelatine, milk and lemon juice, mixing until well blended
- Chill until slightly thickened then fold in whipped cream
- Pour over cracker crumb crust
- Chill until firm
- Top with strawberries before serving

Marbled Cheesecake

Base

1 cup	Graham wafer crumbs
¼ cup	Sugar
¼ cup	Melted butter

- Combine graham cracker crumbs, sugar and melted butter; press on to bottom of 9-inch spring form pan
- Bake at 350° F for 10 minutes

Filling

3 – 8 oz pkg	Cream cheese, softened
¾ cup	Sugar
1 tsp	Vanilla
3	Eggs
1 – 1 oz square	Unsweetened chocolate, melted

- Combine cream cheese, sugar and vanilla, beat at medium speed with electric mixer until well blended
- Add eggs, one at a time, mixing well after each addition
- Blend the melted chocolate into one cup of the batter
- Spoon the white batter and the chocolate batter alternately onto the crust 8" spring form pan.
- Cut through the batter with a knife to create a marbled effect
- Bake at 475°F for 10 minutes
- Lower over heat to 250°F and bake for another 40 minutes
- When cooked, loosen cake from rim of spring form pan, but cool before removing rim completely from the pan.
- Chill for several hours or overnight before serving

Note: Place a pan of water on the bottom rack of the oven while cooking to keep the cheesecake from cracking.

Serves 10 - 12

COOKIES

Smartie Cookies

1 cup	Margarine
2 cups	Brown sugar
2 cups	White sugar
1½ Tbsp	Corn syrup
1½ tsp	Vanilla
3 cups	Peanut butter
4 Tbsp	Baking soda
6	Eggs, well beaten
9 cups	Rolled oats
1 cup	Chocolate chips
2 cups	Smartie candies

- Preheat oven to 350°F
- Cream margarine, brown sugar, white sugar, syrup and vanilla; mix well
- Add peanut butter and baking soda and mix well
- Add well beaten eggs alternately with rolled oats
- Fold in chocolate chips and Smarties
- Drop batter by tablespoon onto a parchment lined cookie sheet
- Bake for 12 minutes or until done

Yield 8 – 10 dozen, depending on the size

Cracker Jack Cookies

1 cup	Butter
1 cup	Brown sugar
1 cup	White sugar
2 tsp	Baking soda
2 tsp	Baking powder
1 tsp	Vanilla
2	Eggs
1 ½ cups	All purpose flour
1 cup	Coconut, medium, unsweetened
2 cups	Rice Krispies
2 cups	Rolled oats

- Preheat oven to 350°F
- Cream butter, white sugar and brown sugar until fluffy
- Add vanilla and eggs, mix well
- Add flour, coconut, Rice Krispies and rolled oats, mix well
- Drop onto parchment lined cookie sheet
- Bake 10 minutes

Yield approximately 3 dozen

Raisin Drops

2 cups	Raisins, washed and squeezed dry
1½ cups	Water
1 cup	Brown sugar
1 cup	Butter
1	Egg
1 tsp	Vanilla
1 tsp	Baking soda
2 tsp	Baking powder
½ tsp	Salt
3 cups	Flour
½ tsp	Ground cloves
¼ tsp	Ground nutmeg
1 tsp	Ground Cinnamon

- Preheat oven to 375°F
- Combine raisins and water and boil for 10 minutes. Set aside to cool, do not drain
- Cream sugar and butter
- Add egg and vanilla, beat well
- Mix dry ingredients together then add to the sugar/butter mixture
- Add raisins and water, mix well
- Drop by teaspoon onto a greased cookie sheet bake for 10 – 12 minutes

Yield approximately 3 dozen

Oatmeal Cookies

1 cup	Butter or margarine
1 cup	Brown sugar
2	Eggs, beaten
½ cup	Sour milk
½ tsp	Cinnamon
¼ tsp	Allspice
½ tsp	Baking soda
½ tsp	Salt
1 1/3 cups	All purpose flour
1 1/3 cups	Rolled oats
1 cup	Chopped nuts (walnuts or pecans)

- Preheat oven to 375°F
- Cream butter and brown sugar well, then add eggs
- Combine dry ingredients together and mix well
- Add dry ingredients to the creamed mixture alternately with the sour milk
- Drop on to parchment lined cookie sheet
- Bake for 10 minutes or until lightly browned
- Cool on cookie sheet

Yield 3 – 4 dozen

Angel Cookies

2½ cups	All purpose flour
1 tsp	Cream of tartar
¾ tsp	Baking soda
½ cup	Margarine
½ cup	Lard or shortening
½ cup	White sugar
½ cup	Brown sugar
1	Egg
1 tsp	Vanilla
½ cup	Walnuts, chopped
	Sugar for coating cookies

- Preheat oven to 375°F
- Measure and sift together flour, cream of tartar and baking soda, set aside
- Beat the margarine, lard or shortening, white and brown sugar, egg and vanilla until fluffy
- Add dry ingredients to creamed mixture then blend in ½ cup chopped walnuts
- Roll into small balls; dip quickly into cold water then roll in sugar
- Place on greased cookie sheet, 2 inches apart; bake for 10 minutes
- Remove immediately from the pan

Yield 1 – 2 dozen

Swiss Tarts

¼ cup	Butter
½ cup	Sugar
1	Egg
1 cup	All purpose flour
½ tsp	Baking powder
½ cup	Cornstarch
1 tsp	Cream of tartar
	Applesauce
	Icing sugar

- Preheat oven to 375°F
- Cream butter and sugar, add egg and beat well
- Add dry ingredients; press together until dough forms a ball (like shortbread)
- Roll out like pastry, to 1/8" thick
- Cut out circles and line small (1" size) tart tins
- Fill each tart with about 1 teaspoon applesauce
- Cut out rounds of pastry to cover applesauce, then seal
- Bake about 10 minutes
- Cool thoroughly
- Sprinkle tarts with icing sugar

Yield 1 dozen

French Cream Puffs

½ cup	Shortening
1 cup	Boiling water
1 cup	All Purpose flour, sifted
1 tsp	Salt
4	Eggs

- Preheat oven to 400°F
- Add shortening to boiling water and bring to a boil
- Add flour and salt all at once, stirring vigorously until a ball forms in the centre of the pan
- Cool slightly, add unbeaten eggs one at a time, beating thoroughly after each addition, mixture should be thick
- Drop from spoon onto slightly greased cookie sheet
- Shape lightly into small mounds
- Bake for 35 minutes
- Turn off the heat
- Open the oven door and leave puffs in the oven another 20 minutes
- Cut top of puffs off, fill with whipped cream
- Replace tops and sprinkle with icing sugar

Yield 12 - 15

Snowballs

1 – 8-oz pkg	Cream cheese, softened
¼ cup	Icing sugar
½ cup	Coconut, medium

- Cream the cream cheese and icing sugar together; Add the coconut
- Roll into balls or roll around a well drained maraschino cherry
- Roll in coconut or icing sugar
- Store in a covered container in the fridge

Yield 2 – 2½ dozen

Shortbread

1 pound	Butter, unsalted
1 cup	Berry sugar
2 cups	All purpose flour
1 cup	Rice flour

- Preheat oven to 300°F
- Sift all the dry ingredients together
- Mix in butter; knead until dough cracks
- Roll into balls and press with a fork
- Bake for 10 minutes or until light in colour

Yield 2 – 3 dozen

Peanut Butter Cookies

1 cup	Butter
1 cup	Peanut butter
¾ cup	Brown sugar
¾ cup	White sugar
2	Eggs, beaten
2 cups	All purpose flour, sifted
2 tsp	Baking soda
¼ tsp	Salt

- Preheat oven to 350°F
- Cream butter and peanut butter together
- Add all the sugar and the well beaten eggs
- Add sifted flour, salt and soda
- Roll into balls, flatten with a fork
- Bake 10 – 15 minutes

Yield 3 – 4 dozen

Ginger Cookies

¾ cup	Shortening
1 cup	White sugar
¼ cup	Molasses
1	Egg
2 cups	Sifted flour all purpose
¼ tsp	Salt
2 tsp	Baking soda
1 tsp	Cinnamon
1 tsp	Cloves
1 tsp	Ginger

- Preheat oven to 375°F
- Grease cookie sheet
- Sift dry ingredients together
- Cream shortening and sugar
- Add molasses and egg
- Beat well
- Add sifted dry ingredients
- Roll into balls, roll balls in sugar
- Flatten with a tumbler dipped in sugar
- Bake 10 – 15 minutes

Yield about 6 dozen

Thimble Cookies

½ cup	Butter
¼ cup	Sugar
1	Egg, separated
1 tsp	Vanilla
1 cup	All purpose flour, sifted
¾ to 1 cup	Walnuts, finely chopped
	Jam or jelly

- Preheat oven to 350°F
- Cream butter, add sugar gradually and mix well
- Add beaten egg yolk, vanilla and flour
- Shape into balls about the size of a walnut
- Dip balls in unbeaten egg white, then roll in finely chopped walnuts
- Dent the centre with a thimble or the end of the handle of a wooden spoon
- Place on greased baking sheet
- Bake for 5 minutes
- Dent again
- Bake 12 – 15 minutes
- Fill with jam or jelly while still hot

Yield 3 – 4 dozen

Brownies

½ cup	Butter
1 cup	White sugar
2	Eggs, beaten
6 Tbsp	Cocoa
1 cup	All purpose flour, sifted
½ cup	Pecans, chopped
1/8 tsp	Salt
½ tsp	Vanilla

- Preheat oven to 325°F
- Cream butter, add sugar and beat until light and fluffy
- Add beaten eggs
- Add cocoa, flour, pecans, salt and vanilla
- Spread like fudge in a greased 8" x 8" cake pan
- Bake in a slow oven for 20 minutes
- Cut in squares while still hot

Yield 16 – 20 squares

Oatcakes

½ cup	Sugar
1 ½ cups	All purpose flour
1 ½ cups	Rolled oats
½ cup	Margarine
½ cup	Shortening
½ tsp	Baking soda
¼ cup	Cold water

- Preheat oven to 400°F
- Mix dry ingredients together
- Cut in the margarine and shortening with a pastry cutter till crumbly
- Add cold water, and mix together until it forms a ball
- Roll out to ¼ inch thick
- Cut into triangles
- Bake for 15 minutes

Yield 1 ½ - 2 dozen

Chinese Chews

¾ cup	All purpose flour, sifted
1 tsp	Baking powder
1 cup	White sugar
¼ tsp	Salt
1 cup	Dates, chopped
1 cup	Walnuts, chopped
2	Eggs, beaten until light
	Icing sugar

- Preheat oven to 350°F
- Sift flour with baking powder, sugar and salt
- Add chopped dates and walnuts
- Add beaten eggs, mix until dough forms
- Spread as thinly as possible in a well greased shallow pan
- Bake for 20 minutes
- When baked, cut into small squares
- Roll squares into balls then roll in icing sugar

Yield 3 – 4 dozen

DESSERTS

Pineapple Dessert

1	Pineapple, peeled, cored and cut into small cubes
½ cup	Icing sugar
3 Tbsp	Cointreau or any other orange liqueur
3 Tbsp	Rum
1 ¼ cups	Heavy cream
3 Tbsp	Kirsch
	Grated rind of one orange

- Pour Cointreau, rum and 6 Tbsp of icing sugar over the pineapple
- Chill in refrigerator for 2 hours
- Whip the cream with remaining sugar,
- Flavour with Kirsch
- Toss the whipped cream and the pineapple together
- Pour into a bowl and sprinkle orange rind over the top
- Serve in a punch bowl or trifle bowl

Serves 4 – 6

Baked Custard

3 large	Eggs
2 cups	Milk
¼ cup	Sugar
1 tsp	Vanilla
1/8 tsp	Salt
	Nutmeg

- Preheat oven to 350°F
- Arrange 6 ramekins or custard cups in a large cake pan
- In a bowl or a large measuring cup, beat together the eggs, milk, sugar, salt and vanilla
- Pour egg/milk mixture through a strainer into the ramekins or cups
- Grate a little nutmeg on top
- Place boiling water around the ramekins to come half way up the cups
- Place in the centre of the oven
- Bake for 35 –40 minutes or until custard is set

Serves 6

Apple Crisp

4 cups	Apples pared and sliced
½ tsp	Cinnamon
1/3 cup	White sugar
2 Tbsp	Water
¼ cup	Butter, softened
¾ cup	Brown sugar
¾ cup	All purpose flour

- Preheat oven to 350°F
- Grease a deep baking dish,
- Arrange sliced apples in layers, sprinkling each layer with cinnamon and sugar.
- Sprinkle water over apples
- Cream butter and gradually add brown sugar and flour
- Spread lightly over the apples
- Bake for 40 – 45 minutes
- Top with whipped cream

Serves 6

Blueberry Apple Crisp

3 cups	Blueberries
3 cups	Apples, peeled and sliced
1 Tbsp	Lemon juice
½ cup	White sugar
1 cup	All purpose flour + 1 Tbsp
1 cup	Brown sugar
1 cup	Rolled oats
1 tsp	Baking powder
1 tsp	Cinnamon
¼ tsp	Salt
½ cup	Butter

- Preheat oven to 350°F
- Combine blueberries and apples in a 11" x 7" baking dish; sprinkle with lemon juice
- Combine white sugar and 1 Tbsp flour, sprinkle over fruit and toss gently
- Combine 1 cup flour, brown sugar, rolled oats, baking powder, cinnamon and salt
- Blend butter into flour mixture to form coarse crumbs; sprinkle over the fruit
- Bake 45 minutes or until apples are done

Serves 6

Raisin Pudding

1 cup	All purpose flour, sifted
½ cup	White sugar
1¾ tsp	Baking powder
½ cup	Raisins
½ cup	Milk
¼ tsp	Salt

- Preheat oven to 350°F
- Sift together flour, sugar, baking powder and salt
- Add raisins and milk and mix gently
- Put batter into a greased casserole

Sauce:

¾ cup	water
½ cup	brown sugar
3 Tbsp	butter

- In a medium saucepan over medium heat mix together water and brown sugar
- Stir until sugar is dissolved
- Add the butter, stir until melted
- Pour sauce over pudding
- Bake for 30 minutes

Serves 6 – 8

Rice Pudding

3 cups	Milk
1 ¼ cup	Rice
¼ cup	White sugar
¼ tsp	Salt
½ tsp	Vanilla
¼ tsp	Cinnamon
½ cup	Raisins

- Preheat oven to 350°F
- Mix all ingredients together
- Pour mixture into a buttered oven proof casserole
- Bake for 2 hours or until rice is tender
- Cover casserole for the first hour

Serves: 6

Quick Delicious Pudding

1 cup	All purpose flour
1/3 cup	Brown sugar
¼ tsp	Salt
1½ tsp	Baking powder
1 cup	Raisins
1 Tbsp	Butter
2/3 cup	Milk

- Preheat oven to 350°F
- Sift flour, sugar, salt and baking powder
- Rub in the butter
- Add raisins and milk to make a soft dough
- Turn into a well greased baking dish

Sauce:

1 cup	Brown sugar
¼ tsp	Salt
2 tsp	Vanilla
1 Tbsp	Butter
2 cups	Boiling water

- Mix all ingredients together and pour over the dough; Bake for ½ hour

Serves 6

Rhubarb Pudding

3 cups	Rhubarb, cut into approx ¾ " slices
3 Tbsp	Water
¾ cup	Sugar
1 Tbsp	Tapioca
2	Eggs
1/8 tsp	Salt
¼ tsp	Cream of tartar
6 Tbsp	Sugar
¼ tsp	Vanilla
6 Tbsp	Flour

- Preheat oven to 350°F
- Place rhubarb, water, sugar and tapioca in an 8x8 casserole
- Beat eggs, salt and cream of tartar until very light
- Add sugar gradually
- Add vanilla, fold in flour
- Pour over rhubarb
- Bake for 40 minutes

Serves 6 – 8

Bread Pudding

2 cup	Milk
4 cups	Cubed, stale bread
1 cup	Brown sugar
1/3 cup	Butter, melted
2	Eggs
2 tsp	Vanilla
1 cup	Raisins, washed and drained
1 cup	Dried cranberries
½ tsp	Cinnamon

- Preheat oven to 350°F
- In a mixing bowl, add milk to the bread
- In a separate bowl, combine remaining ingredients beating well, then add to the bread mixture
- Pour into a buttered, oven proof casserole
- Bake for 50 – 60 minutes
- Serve with whipped cream

Serves 6 - 8

Chocolate Mousse

½ pound	Sweet bakers chocolate
5	Eggs, separated
1 cup	Heavy cream, whipped
1 Tbsp	Orange liqueur
3 Tbsp	Strong coffee

- Melt chocolate in a double boiler over hot, not boiling, water, cool
- Beat egg yolks until thick and lemon coloured, add liqueur and coffee
- Combine with the chocolate and blend until smooth
- Beat egg whites until stiff
- Fold carefully into the chocolate mixture
- Fold whipped cream into the mixture and spoon into glasses or greased moulds

Serves 8 – 10

PIES
& PASTRY

Pie Pastry

5 cups	All purpose flour
½ tsp	Baking soda
2 Tbsp	Sugar
2 tsp	Salt
1 pound	Shortening
1	Egg
3 tsp	Vinegar
	Cold water

- Place flour, baking soda, sugar and salt in a large bowl, mix well
- Break shortening into medium pieces; add to dry ingredients
- Break egg into a 1-cup measure, add vinegar and beat together
- Fill with cold water to 1 cup
- Pour over flour mixture
- Mix until a ball starts to form in the bowl
- Turn out onto a generously floured board
- Knead and turn and mix until it shapes itself into around ball
- Wrap tightly in plastic and refrigerate until ready to use
- Makes enough for 3 double-crust pies

Apple Pie

5 – 6 large	Apples, peeled and cored
1 cup	Sugar
3½ Tbsp	Flour
1½ Tbsp	Lemon juice
¼ tsp	Allspice
¼ tsp	Cinnamon
Dash	Salt
2 Tbsp	Butter
	Pastry, enough for bottom and top crust

- Preheat oven to 425°F
- Put apples in large bowl; add sugar, lemon juice, flour, cinnamon, allspice & salt
- Toss together and let stand while rolling out the pastry, stirring a few times
- Pour the apple mixture into the bottom crust dot with butter
- Brush edge of bottom crust with water
- Cover with the top crust, seal and crimp
- Gently brush the top crust with milk
- Cut steam vents and sprinkle with sugar
- Bake for 30 minutes at 425°F, then lower temperature to 350°F and bake another 30 – 40 minutes, cool completely

Serves 6 - 8

Rhubarb Pie

3 Tbsp	Flour
1 ½ cups	Sugar
1	Egg, beaten
2 ½ cups	Rhubarb, cut into small pieces
	Pastry, enough for bottom and top crust

- Preheat oven to 425°F
- Sift flour and sugar together and add egg
- Beat well then add rhubarb
- Line 9-inch pie pan with pastry
- Pour in the filling
- Cover with top crust; seal and crimp
- Cut several steam vents
- Brush with milk and sprinkle with sugar
- Bake for 15 minutes at 425°F then lower oven temperature to 350°F and bake an additional 35 – 45 minutes

Serves 6 - 8

Peach Pie

1 cup	Sugar
3 Tbsp	Flour
¼ tsp	Salt
8	Peaches, peeled and sliced
2 Tbsp	'Surefresh' or lemon juice
	Pastry, enough for bottom and top crust

- Preheat oven to 425°F
- Sprinkle the sliced peaches with 'Surefresh' or lemon juice (this keeps the peaches from darkening)
- Sift dry ingredients together then mix with the peaches
- Line a 9-inch pie plate with pastry
- Fill with the peach mixture
- Cover with top crust; seal and crimp
- Cut in steam vents
- Brush with milk and sprinkle with sugar
- Bake at 425°F for 30 minutes
- Slip a baking pan beneath the pie pan and reduce the oven temperature to 350°F and bake a further 30 - 35 minutes

Serves 6 - 8

Blueberry Pie

4 cups	Blueberries, washed and dried
1 cup	Sugar
¼ cup	Flour
¼ tsp	Salt
1 ½ Tbsp	Lemon juice
	Pastry, enough for bottom and top crust

- Preheat oven to 450°F
- Mix berries with sugar, salt flour and lemon juice
- Line a 9 - inch pie plate with pastry
- Pour in filling
- Cover with top crust; seal and crimp
- Crimp and cut several steam vents
- Brush top with milk and sprinkle with sugar
- Bake at 450°F for 10 minutes.
- Reduce oven temperature to 350°F and bake another 30 – 35 minutes

Serves 6 - 8

CoConut Cream Pie

1¾ cups	Milk
¼ cup	Sugar
¼ tsp	Salt
3 Tbsp	Flour
2	Egg yolks, beaten
1 Tbsp	Butter
½ tsp	Vanilla
1½ cups	Shredded coconut
	Whipped cream
1¾ cups	Fine graham crumbs
¼ cup	Sugar
½ cup	Butter, melted

- Mix the crumbs and sugar together stir in the melted butter
- Line the bottom and sides of a 9-inch pie plate with the mixture by pressing it firmly in place
- Bake in a 350°F oven for 10 minutes, cool
- Scald 1 cup milk over boiling water
- Mix the sugar, salt, flour and remaining milk together then stir into hot milk and cook slowly until thickened, stirring constantly
- Cover and cook over boiling water for 5 minutes
- VERY slowly add the beaten egg yolks to the hot mixture stirring constantly. Cook one minute longer then add butter and vanilla
- Stir in coconut, cool then pour into crumb pie shell
- Spread with whipped cream

Serves 8 - 10

Flapper Pie

1 1/4 cups	Graham wafer crumbs
1/4 cup	Sugar
1/3 cup	Melted butter
1/2 cup	Sugar
2 Tbsp	Corn starch
1 Tbsp	Flour
1/4 tsp	Salt
2 cups	Milk
2	Egg yolks, beaten
1 Tbsp	Butter
1 tsp	Vanilla
2	Egg whites
1/4 cup	Sugar

- Preheat oven to 375°F
- Combine crumbs, sugar and butter well
- Reserve 1/4 cup of the crumb mixture for topping
- Press the remaining crumbs in a 9-inch pie plate
- Bake for 8 minutes, cool
- In a microwave bowl combine, the next 5 ingredients, cook until mixture bubbles and thickens, stirring after every minute
- Stir a little of the hot mixture into the egg yolks
- Put remaining yolks into the mixture cook for 1 minute
- Blend in butter and vanilla, cool for 10 minutes and pour over crumb crust, cool
- Top with meringue topping

Meringue Topping: Beat egg whites until soft peaks form. Slowly add the sugar. Beat until stiff and shiny. Spread over cooled filling, sprinkle with reserved crumbs. Bake in 425°F oven for 5 minutes. Cool and serve.

Pumpkin Pie

	Pastry, for bottom crust
1/8 tsp	Salt
2/3 cup	Sugar
2 tsp	Pumpkin pie spice
2	Eggs, slightly beaten
1 2/3 cups	Milk
1½ cups	Pumpkin, cooked & mashed

- Preheat oven to 450°F
- Sift dry ingredients together; add eggs
- Add milk and pumpkin
- Line a pie plate with pastry, pour in filling
- Bake at 450°F for 10 minutes
- Reduce heat to 325°F and bake 35 minutes longer or until a knife inserted in the centre comes out clean

Serves 6 - 8

158

PRESERVES

Mincemeat

4 cups	Green tomatoes, peeled, minced and drained
2 cups	Prune plums, minced
6 cups	Apples, unpeeled, minced
1 pound	Raisins, washed and drained
1 pound	Currants, washed and drained
4 cups	Sugar
1 tsp	Cinnamon
2 tsp	Allspice
2 tsp	Cloves
½ cup	Vinegar

- In a large pot, mix all ingredients together and bring to a boil
- Simmer for one hour, stirring frequently
- Fill prepared jars and process for 15 minutes

Yield (4 – 6 pint jars)

Antipasto

2 pounds	Cauliflower, cut in small pieces
1 pound	Pickling onions, chopped in small pieces
2 cans	Mushrooms, chopped
2 cans	Green beans, cut in small pieces
2 cans	Black olives, cut in small pieces
2 12 oz jars	Green olives, cut in small pieces
2 – 7-oz cans	Tuna, chopped
1 – 12-oz jar	Dill pickles, chopped
2 pounds	Green peppers, seeded and chopped
2 pounds	Red peppers, seeded and chopped
1¾ cups	Olive oil
1½ litre	Ketchup
1¾ cups	Vinegar
3½ cups	Tomato sauce

- In a very large pot, combine all ingredients.
- Bring to a boil, simmer for 30 minutes
- Put into sterilized jars, process 25 minutes

Green Tomato Sandwich Spread

1 quart	Chopped green tomatoes
1 cup	Chopped onions
1 medium	Green peppers, chopped
3 medium	Red peppers, chopped
½ cup	Pickling salt
1 cup	Water
7 Tbsp	Flour
1 ½ cups	White sugar
2 tsp	Mustard
1 cup	Vinegar
2 cups	Sour cream
3	Eggs
1 cup	Chopped sweet pickles

- Wash tomatoes, chop in a processor and measure out 1 quart
- Peel onions and chop
- Chop peppers and add to tomatoes and onions
- Sprinkle with pickling salt
- Allow to stand for 4 hours, drain well
- Add 1 cup of water to drained vegetables, cook until tender but not soft
- Add chopped sweet pickle and keep mixture warm while preparing the dressing
- Mix flour, sugar and mustard add cold vinegar to make a paste
- Add sour cream gradually then well beaten eggs
- Cook in a double boiler until thick, stirring constantly
- Pour hot dressing over vegetable and stir until well mixed
- Pour into hot sterilized jars and process for 15 minutes

Pickled Onions

5 pounds	Pickling onions, peeled
1 cup	Pickling salt
2 quarts	Boiling water

- Place onions in a large glass bowl, cover with the salt and boiling water,
- Let stand for 2 days, then drain
- Pack the onions into sterilized jars
- Fill jars with the following syrup
    - 1 quart vinegar
    - 5 – 6 cups sugar
    - 1 Tbsp pickling spice
- Boil for 3 – 5 minutes and pour over the onions and process for 10 minutes

Pickled Eggs

2 dozed	Hard boiled eggs, peeled and chilled
2½ cups	White vinegar
3 Tbsp	Sugar
2 tsp	Salt
2 Tbsp	Pickling spice (in cheesecloth bag)
2 cups	Cold water

- Combine vinegar, sugar, salt spices and water
- Boil for 10 minutes, cool then pour over eggs
- Let stand for 3 days before using

Pickled Beets

4 pounds	Small beets, cooked and skinned
3 cups	Beet water, strained
2 cups	Cider vinegar
1 cup	Brown sugar
	Whole cloves

- Boil the beets until done, reserve the water
- Bring the vinegar, 3 cups of the strained beet water, brown sugar and the beets to a boil
- Cook for 5 minutes
- Pack the beets in sterilized jars
- Fill with the boiling liquid to within ½ inch of the top
- Process in a hot water bath for 20 – 25 minutes

Red Pepper Jelly

5 - 6	Red sweet peppers
5 ½ cups	Sugar
1 bottle	Certo
1 cup	Diluted vinegar (1/2 water: 1/2 vinegar)
1/3 cup	Lemon juice

- Wash peppers, remove seeds and process until fine
- Place peppers, sugar and diluted vinegar in a pot
- Heat rapidly to a boil, stirring constantly
- Remove from heat
- Let stand for 15 minutes
- Reheat to boiling, add lemon juice
- Boil for 2 minutes
- Remove from heat, add Certo
- Stir for 5 minutes
- Pour into sterilized jars
- Process for 10 minutes

Note: If a spicier jelly is wanted, just add about ¼ - ½ tsp of hot pepper flakes before boiling. This recipe can also be made with green peppers; follow the same method.

Recipe list

168